HOW 'BOUT THEM COWBOYS!

by Frank Coffey & Ernie Wood
with Tony Seidl

Taylor Publishing Company
Dallas, Texas

All books are written, edited, designed and produced by group effort; the following people made important contributions to a project executed with unusual time pressures. The authors would like to thank Lynn Brooks, Arnie Hanson, Jim Donovan and Carol Trammel, the able folks at Taylor Publishing; editor/writers extraordinaire John Pynchon Holms, Wayne Coffey, Carl Waldman and Aleksandrs Rozens; and the production team at Pink Coyote Designs, Inc.—Pat Reshen, Joel Ponzan, Alan Blaustein and Eduardo Andino.

The photography in this book was accomplished by a talented trio: Layne Murdoch, Lewis DeLuca and A. Kaye Photo. Without their stunning images our story would have been paler indeed.

Published by Taylor Publishing Company
1550 West Mockingbird Lane
Dallas, Texas 75235

ISBN: 0-87833-827-6 paperback
0-87833-828-4 hardback

Designed by Joel Ponzan & Eduardo Andino, Pink Coyote Designs, Inc.

Printed in the United States of America
10 9 8 7 6 5 4 3 2 1

CONTENTS

How 'Bout Them 'Boys!

America's team is back. Covered with glory. On the last day of January 1993, 120 million people watched a new Dallas Cowboy team create the next generation's heroes.

Led by Jimmy Johnson, directed by Super Bowl MVP Troy Aikman and starring Emmitt Smith and Michael Irvin, these 'Boys have written their names in football history.

The embarrassment of 1989, just recently a blink of the eye away, seems long, long ago. An ugly past that now, suddenly, history will see as prologue. To triumph.

Haley and Norton. Everett and Novacek. The fresh, new names will, in time, resonate powerfully, will remind today's young—and young at heart—of 1993's sweet and special times. Once veterans like Lilly and Renfro, Howley and Jordan were revered for their accomplishments, for how they played the game. Today there are additions to that Hall of Memory. Veterans Jim Jeffcoat and Mark Tuinei, who knew the good times and the bad. Injured stalwart Bill Bates, a big part of this team's heart. Jimmie Jones, a part of its future. Tony Casillas and James Washington, Alvin Harper and Kelvin Martin. Daryl Johnston. Mark Stepnoski, Russell Maryland, and big Nate Newton. Emerging star ErikWilliams and veterans Ken Norton and Ike Holt. John Gesek and Kevin Gogan and Tony Tolbert.

In the grand old dynasty days this glorious 1992 season would have been greeted with satisfaction. And, certainly, with pleasure. But, mostly, it would have been accepted as the natural order of things. A birth right. The Cowboys win. Of course. And the sun also rises.

This year's upstart Dallas Cowboy team provokes a different kind of response. Whoops and hollers. This team feels like family. We feel affection. Pride. And ain't it wonderful!

The Landry Cowboys were cool, efficient, almost aloof. This Jimmy Johnson team is young, emotional and, well... in your face. A combination of hip-hop and country and western, as fast with a quip as they are on their feet. Flamboyant. Fresh. The real deal. A blast to watch and root for.

It has been said that we never appreciate what we have until we lose it. This explains, in part, the raw, wild enthusiasm for the "new" Cowboys. The rest is supplied by coach Jimmy Johnson and his brash troops. The credo is simple: Go for it. Don't hold back. Take chances. If we lose—which isn't happening much anymore—lose by trying to win. Don't ever be afraid to take a risk. Don't ever be afraid of losing.

Good Lord, has ever a philosophy worked better?

Tragedy, the old aphorism goes, is not so much what one suffers, but what one misses. By that definition, the Cowboy fans have known tragedy. By 1992, they were ready to embrace the good times again. Finally, the long nightmare is over.

There is something pure, almost innocent about this Cowboy team. They arrived at the pinnacle of pro football before their notoriety was established. Their major opponents in the playoffs, the 49ers and Bills, were full of legends, their stories remarkable, but familiar.

The Cowboys represent the unknown. Brash newcomers who refuse to be denied. Yes, they possess stars, but more than individuals they are a unit. Cohesive, driven, talented. A team.

"For all you players and coaches," Jimmy Johnson told them on national television after their Super Bowl victory, "hey, understand this: As much as you relish being the best, as much as you relish that and as good as it feels, the best thing that you've got and what you'll have the rest of your lives is the love that you got from one another. Because that's what got you here—being a total team. And that feeling is something you'll never ever lose. It'll be the greatest feeling in the world. Hey! Congratulations!"

Ernie Wood
Austin, Texas

Frank Coffey
New York

January 31, 1993

A GLORIOUS PAST

THE EARLY YEARS: 1960-70

Great moments in sport are created by players and captured by fans...relished in the instant and savored in the remembering and retelling. Legends are made through the feats of gifted, daring athletes, who achieve immortality in the memory of those who were fortunate enough to be witnesses.

Football is a game that

Bowl rings—wasn't an easy one. But such roads rarely are. Many teams never make the journey at all. Certainly, before the mid-'50s and network television, even the great teams played more for the guts and glory and love of the game than the security that success could bring. But, by the late fifties, the raw courage and dedication shown by those early champions was about to pay off.

Professional football seized the hearts and minds of Americans forever in December of 1958 when the Baltimore Colts beat the New York

demands greatness. No team has delivered more of what the game demands than the Dallas Cowboys. Great plays, great players...greatness, pure and simple. From 1966, with their first of 20 consecutive winning seasons, to 1985, the Cowboys were a force to be reckoned with in the NFL.

The road to glory—the road that led to 13 division championships, five NFC titles and two Super

Giants 23-17 for the National Championship. Frenzied fans rocked Yankee Stadium, while millions of people all over the country sat glued to their televisions watching what was undoubtedly one of the great football games of all time.

After almost 30 years of organized league play, a passion and excitement for the game had finally gripped fans with a fervor

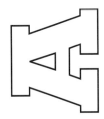

equaling that of the dedicated and long-suffering men who played and coached in relative obscurity... men happy just to have the chance to be part of the game they loved. Sunday afternoons in the fall would never be the same.

The owners knew it, the players knew it and the fans knew it. A fresh wind was blowing, with expansion in the air. Fate was about to bring together three very different men, sending them down a road to glory that was then little more than a two-lane blacktop disappearing into the endless distance of the dusty Texas plains. Tom Landry, Tex Schramm and Gil

that was unstable at best. A five-year contract had persuaded him to give Dallas a try.

On January 28, 1960, Clint Murchison, Jr., heir to an oil and real estate fortune, and his partner Bedford Wynne were awarded the franchise by the NFL, and Schramm, Landry and Brandt set about the business of building a competitive team from the leftovers and rejects garnered from the rest of the league. It was almost February and the Cowboys first preseason game, against the San Francisco 49ers, was scheduled for August 6, 1960.

As if the task of fielding a brand new team in a few short months

Bill Bates, whose 1992 season ended with an October injury, remained an important part of the team as one of the last links between past and present.

Texas Stadium opened fittingly on October 24, 1971 with a 44-21 Cowboy victory over the New England Patriots. Duane Thomas scored the first TD on a 56-yard run. 65,708 fans were in attendance.

Brandt...household names now, but back then...

The journey began on December 28, 1959, at a press conference called by newly hired president Tex Schramm to announce that the Dallas Rangers would be the first team added to the NFL since the merger with the AAFL in 1950. The new head coach would be a young man who had played and later coached the defense for the great New York Giant teams of the '50s. His name was Tom Landry. Schramm also announced that Gil Brandt would become head of personnel. Landry, only the day before, had been wondering if he could gamble his future and the security of his family on a career

wasn't enough of a problem, the fledgling Cowboys were faced with some stiff competition right in their own back yard. Millionaire Lamar Hunt, angry that he couldn't get a team in the NFL, bought a whole damn league and plunked his upstart AFL Dallas Texans right down in the middle of the Cotton Bowl. The Texans were to be a thorn in the Cowboys' side until 1963, when Hunt moved the team to Kansas City and renamed them the Chiefs.

Somehow Landry and his staff managed to get 40 men on the field for the season opener in 1960. Quarterback Eddie LeBaron was coaxed out of retirement to add a little stability, and he played with

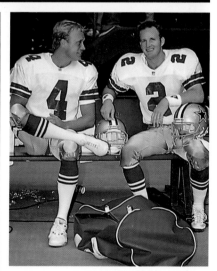

Punter Mike Saxon knew the bad times, rookie Lin Elliott only the good.

Six-foot seven-inch, 317-pound Kevin Gogan was a guard in the dark years, a tackle in the glory season of '92.

good humor and a lot of grit. He needed it. Remember Bob Fry? John Gonzaga? Buzz Guy? Maybe their moms and sweethearts do, but no one else. The Cowboys went 0-11-1 in their first season, the only bright spot being a 31-31 tie with Landry's old team, the Giants. The good news, however, was that a system was being put in place by the coaching staff and front office that would serve them well down the stretch. Even before the franchise was secure they had signed a young quarterback out of Southern Methodist named Don Meredith and a strong prospect out of New Mexico named Don Perkins. A little light at the end of the long, dark tunnel.

The Cowboys put their first win on the board in the '61 season opener, whipping Pittsburgh 27-24. They went on to win four more games and draft the soon-to-be-legendary Bob Lilly. A future seven-time All-Pro and Hall-of-Famer, Lilly was the signal that the system Schramm, Landry and Brandt were forging was working.

Still, by the end of the '63 season, the Cowboys weren't winners, and if you ain't a winner in Texas you're all hat and no cattle. With a 13-38-2 record, there were rumblings that Landry was in trouble. In possibly the smartest football move of all time, Clint Murchison offered him a 10-year contract, and although no one, with the possible exception of the owner and his president, knew it then, the dynasty was born. Landry would later say, "That was the most significant thing that ever happened to me."

Meredith, who played hurt or healthy and always with a lot of courage, and six-time Pro Bowler Perkins took the Cowboys to their first winning season and their first NFL Championship Game in 1966. Even though they lost a tough one to Lombardi's Packers, 34-27, the 10-3 season marked the beginning of a record 20-year winning streak and 18 trips to the playoffs.

The Cowboys roared back in '67 and played the Packers for the championship on a sheet of ice called Lambeau Field. Enduring frigid temperatures and arctic winds, the teams fought to the final seconds. The Packers pulled out the "Ice Bowl" 21-17. A defeat for the 'Boys, yes. But in some defeats, there's a special kind of victory. Texans will tell you that on the frozen turf of the north country, the seeds of America's Team were sown.

The '68 season seemed a dream come true for Dallas fans. Dandy Don was at his peak on and off the field. Although injured, he took the team to 12-2, and the Cowboys seemed poised to taste the fruits of victory. It was not to be. The Browns crushed them 31-20 in the Eastern Championship Game, and there was little consolation in winning the Playoff Bowl over Miami 17-13.

But things were falling into place. The blueprint for success had been drawn up right. Murchison had hired the best people he could find and let them alone to do their work. And homework they did. The '64 Cowboy draft had been a bumper crop, one of the best ever, with soon-to-be greats Mel Renfro, Bob Hayes, Chuck Howley, Lee Roy Jordan and a talented future draft choice by the name of Roger Staubach. Staubach did not join the team until 1969, after completing his naval career. But until his retirement in 1980, "Mr. Comeback" would lead Dallas to six NFC Championship games and four Super Bowls, winning two.

Because the Cowboys were now consistent winners, the odds on getting quality players out of the draft weren't good. The trifecta was forced to develop a rating system to root out the talent that everybody else missed, then negotiate for position to get them. They did it brilliantly. Draft and trade. Trade and draft. Knock Tex's computer if you dare...but it produced stalwarts such as Dennis Thurman, Jean Fugett, Larry Cole and Jethro Pugh. The '75 draft alone reaped Randy White, Hollywood Henderson, Scott Laidlaw, Randy Hughes, Herb Scott and Mike Hegman. How about Drew "Hail Mary" Pearson? Danny White? Preparation the key to success? No kidding.

"I feel like I'm part of the legacy."
–Jim Jeffcoat

Ten-year veteran Jim Jeffcoat has played more Dallas games than any current Cowboy.

The Top of the Mountain: 1971-85

The Glory Years speak for themselves. The records are in the books, sustained flashes of brilliance captured on film and tape and, of course, in the mind's eye of millions of spectators. Super Bowl Rings and Conference Championships. Games won and lost. Close contests and runaways. Great plays and great courage. The extra effort, giving just a little more, playing tough, playing every down, never giving up.

The Cowboys of Landry and Staubach and Lilly and all the rest won with skill and courage. Preparation and inspired play. They won by solid execution and by pulling rabbits out of hats. Whatever it took. No game was over as long as the Cowboys could get the ball. And the Doomsday Defense made other teams wonder if somebody was leaking game plans. The Cowboys just got the job done, over and over again. They made you mad and you could never seem to get even. Save for their Super Bowl nemesis the Pittsburgh Steelers, in a league of giants they seemed just a little bit taller and broader then the rest. They came at you like a stampede, or a runaway freight train, and you could feel the ground tremble and maybe know just a little fear. In fact, they rarely lost a game. They just ran out of clock.

And then it was over.

Decline: A Chilly Wind

Dallas won its 13th division title in 1985 but lost to the Rams in the playoffs. Something was different. Due to ill health, Murchison had sold the team in 1984 to oilman H.R. "Bum" Bright. By the late '80s, the core of the team was aging dramatically. Randy White, Ed Jones, Doug Cosbie, Tom Rafferty and quarterback Danny White were at the end of their careers. John Dutton, Tony Hill, Mike Hegman and Ron Fellows had retired. Tailback legend Tony Dorsett was gone. The coach had started running the team when its new star running back, Herschel Walker, was two years old. Bright young assistants like Dan Reeves, Gene Stallings, Mike Ditka and John Mackovic had long since departed. And the current coaching staff, including Ernie Stautner, Jerry Tubbs and Dick Nolan, had held their jobs since the mid-1960s.

A noble line of quarterbacks—Eddie LeBaron, Don Meredith, Roger Staubach and Danny White—had no heir. Steve Pelluer? Many felt he had more courage than talent, so regularly was he knocked out while running. "I'm out there to get first downs," Pelluer said, "not run out of bounds." Pelluer's replacement,

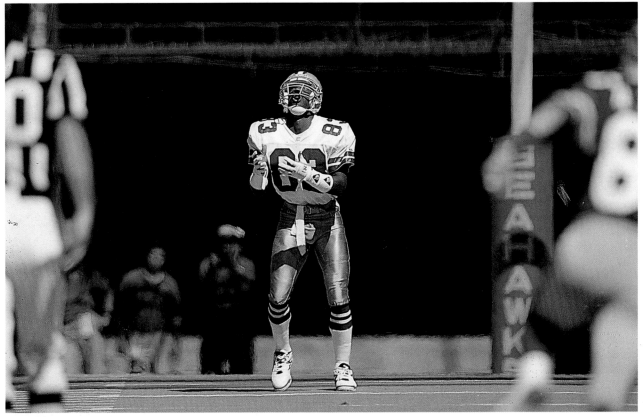

Swift Kelvin Martin is one of 16 remaining Cowboys from the dreadful 1989 team to reach the Super Bowl mountaintop.

Kevin "His Shortness" Sweeney, said after a 43-3 wipeout by Minnesota, "I'm not the savior." No one disagreed. Instead of a fond memory, Don Meredith to "Bullet" Bob Hayes seemed like ancient history. Offensive tackle Crawford Ker described the state of the 1988 Dallas Cowboys by stating, "You can't get any lower than this."

Ker was wrong.

The Cowboys were in rapid decline. Landry was receiving criticism for personally coaching the defense, as well as making play calls for the offense. As the record tumbled from 7-8 to 3-13, the worst in the NFL, it was becoming apparent that even brilliant coach Tom Landry couldn't cure the team's ills. And Bright, who had suffered huge loses in the market crash of '87, was feeling restless as he watched his investment go from bad to worse.

The scene was set for change. Huge, generational change. It was no secret that Bright was looking for a buyer. Nor was Bright a hands-off owner like Murchison; by 1987, he was publicly criticizing Landry's conservative offense, at one point calling his coach's choices "horrendous." Another time Bright said: "It doesn't seem like we've got anybody in charge that knows what they're doing, other than Tex."

By March of 1988, the Cowboys were for sale. In November, rumors were rampant that oil mogul Marvin Davis was about to purchase the franchise. An unnamed Japanese billionaire (undoubtedly interested in the America's Team label), a group of Canadian investors, and Los Angeles Lakers owner Jerry Buss were also mentioned. Formal bids were made by Edward Smith, Jr., a 27% owner in the Cowboys, and Donald Carter, owner of the NBA's Dallas Mavericks. But it was another entrepreneur, an oil, banking and real-estate tycoon—and former college football player—named Jerral W. "Jerry" Jones who would claim the prize. (Jones was the majority owner; five minority owners included Smith, Charles, Sam and Evan Wily, who are associated with the Bonanza Steakhouse chain, and Russell Glass.)

The February 1989 announce-

It was hard for many fans to put on a happy face during the hard times.

ment of Jones's purchase of the Cowboys and Texas Stadium omitted the price tag; when it was revealed, the $140 million shocked many. (Bright had paid $60 million for the team, and an additional $25 million for the stadium lease, in 1984). More and bigger shocks were forthcoming.

Tom Landry, the only coach the Cowboys ever had, was being replaced by Jimmy Johnson, the new owners' former teammate and roommate at the University of Arkansas. (And their wives were sorority sisters.)

The uproar was enormous and immediate. In professional sport, never had a more successful head coach been fired. Bum Bright best described what happened: "This is a new generation of ownership, of coaches. It must evolve. That happens and it's part of life. It happens in every business. It's a fact of life."

Veteran defensive back Charlie Waters summed up the end of an era another way: "I never realized how lucky I was to play on such great teams. We were really great. At the time, I didn't think about it. I just played. Now, seeing how things have gone, I feel very fortunate."

The torch had been passed; an era was over. Schramm and Brandt departed shortly after Landry. They had reached the end of that dusty blacktop road they'd set off on 30 years before, and now found themselves heading into different sunsets. Whatever they were feeling at the time, they knew damn well it had been a great ride—and none of them would have changed a thing about it.

Finishing first became a happy habit.

15

JERRY JONES: RAZORBACK TO THE RESCUE

Jerry Jones is much too busy to listen to Garth Brooks or Randy Travis. No time for that. Music to his ears is the happy sounds fans are once again making about the Cowboys.

Take, for example, Melissa Bentley, the wife of a dedicated fan who was giving birth the day of the NFC championship game against San Francisco. "I'm glad that the baby was born in time for my husband to watch the game. It's making him happy."

Now that, for Jerry Jones, is sweet music.

Jerral Wayne Jones, like many driven, ambitious men started from relatively humble beginnings. Born on October 13, 1942, in Los Angeles, his father, J.W. "Pat" Jones, moved the family back home after World War II and opened a fruit stand in Little Rock, Arkansas. He built that into a small group of supermarkets, and then started one of the earliest chains of drive-in markets, Pat's Kwik Check Superettes.

Jones's father, with whom he was extraordinarily close, was a great salesman. "I learned to always be positive," Jones told Playboy magazine, "and I learned

that being positive isn't something that just happens. It's something you decide."

He also learned that if you're a real salesman, you don't wait for money to come to you.

Jerry Jones, a fullback at North Little Rock High School, was turned into a 185-pound guard at Arkansas by coach Frank Broyles. "He just accepted it and went on about his business," Broyles remembered. "He was successful for us because he used his head and he had guts." On that team Jones became friendly with another small lineman; the relationship with Texan Jimmy Johnson would ultimately change both their lives.

After college, Jones went to work for his father's new company, Modern Security Life Insurance. In 1970, the company was sold and Jones had himself a $500,000 grubstake.

He moved on to the gas-and-oil exploration business. Jones's first 13 wells hit gas, and the future Cowboy owner was on his way to building a fortune that would reach $200 million by the time he bought the Dallas franchise.

Jones has a guileless, almost innocent side. When he first visited

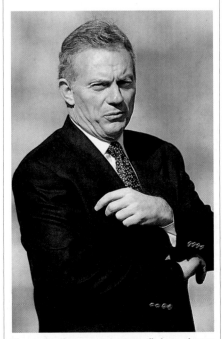

"I want to be a great owner," Jerry Jones said upon buying the Cowboys. So far, so good.

the Cowboy complex he said, "I walked around with my jaw dropped all day." It wasn't long after that he bought it.

That's when the cowpie hit the fan. "When we took over this franchise," Jones says, "we were excited about the future. And it looked like we were disrespectful of the past. That's behind us now. I feel I'm on the right side of the fence here, the right side of the cause in trying to make this work."

But it wasn't that way at the beginning. The team's play-by-play radio voice, Brad Sham, thought Jones was "a man who's taken more abuse than any person I've ever known."

That's what happens when you fire "God's Coach," when you let a legend go. The conversation in which Jones fired Landry remains a difficult memory. Jones called it "a very awkward and trying thing. It's the most inadequate I've ever been in my life. If you had graded my conversation, I would have gotten an 'F.'" (To be honest, some Cowboys from earlier years said, with some bitterness, that Landry had gotten the same heartless treatment he had meted out.)

"We knew it was a very difficult

thing because of what Tom Landry meant to the Dallas Cowboys, but we just felt we had to go in another direction," Jones said. "Maybe we could have handled it better at the time, but sometimes things happen like that. It was not an easy decision."

"Tom Landry is like Bear Bryant to me," Jones said of the 64-year-old coach. "He's Vince Lombardi to me. If you love competitors, he's an angel. Tom Landry is the Cowboys, and just like Tex Schramm is the Cowboys. But let me tell you this, Jimmy Johnson would be the first to tell you he couldn't carry Tom's waterbucket."

Looking back, Tex Schramm thinks maybe the "difficult" situation was handled all right after all. "Maybe it all was the best thing that could have happened to Tom [Landry] and myself. It might have happened a little too quickly, but as it turned out Tom had an opportunity to go out with a lot of class and with people showing a lot of feeling for him. He became a hero again to everybody, even to those who had been so critical of him...and with both of us gone, it closed out an era."

The first response from the public wasn't easy to take. Critics called him "Jethro" Jones, the Hillbilly of Valley Ranch. A cold-hearted, ruthless mogul. And worse. Jones's daughter Charlotte, recalls her father's reaction to the hostility: "That first year, my mom and brother and I just couldn't believe how strong he was. He just kept telling us that we had to understand how much this team meant to people and that it would take a while for them to accept any kind of change."

But Jones hung tough. He and his wife, Gene, moved the family to Dallas. "I kept saying over and over again, 'We're here to stay,'" Jones said. "I didn't buy the Cowboys to make money. I had money."

And make no mistake, Jones is no football dilettante. The Cowboys are not a hobby, the way other rich men take up, say, polo. "Everything I've done in my life, I put on the line with this team," said Jones.

"I'm going to examine each facet of the organization," Jones said. "The Cowboys will be my life." He claimed he'd be involved with everything from "socks to jocks." The man was as good as his promise.

Asked about the price of the team, Jones said, "That's between Bum and me, but I don't mind telling you I'm going to need some lead in my back pocket. I'm going to leave Dallas lighter than when I came in."

A Texas field of dreams.

Doubtless, this is true. Now, however, with the Cowboys flying high, the bank accounts are filled with black. Attendance in 1991 was the highest since the Glory Years, over 62,000 fans per game, and 1992 season subscriptions topped 46,000. The NFL blackout is again history, so all Cowboy games are back on local television. The team is, perhaps, the most highly recognized, best-marketed team in pro sports. Amazingly, the team puts out a weekly newspaper, which has subscribers in 33 countries. And Spanish-speaking audiences in the U.S. and abroad will see live coverage of the Super Bowl for the third consecutive year.

Jones has tirelessly promoted his Dallas team. Cowboys revenues are up $30 million in total during his four-year tenure.

"You knew he was going to become a compelling and important figure in sports because he knew sports was entertainment," powerful agent Leigh Steinberg told the Associated Press. "And he knew that to entertain, you had to win."

Regarding the past and the awkward way the Jerry Jones era began, the owner says: "The best thing we can do for Coach Landry and for the Cowboy fans who have been with us from day one, 31 years ago, is to do everything we can to put these Cowboys on the lips of everybody that is interested in sports by going to the Super Bowl." Jones said this in October 1992…little did he know how soon his prophecy would come true. "I don't feel we have attained the level of success that is expected of us or I would have expected."

Well, the owner has won far more and far faster than he or anyone could have predicted. The future is now.

Jones's son Stephen recently spoke revealingly to writer Mike Lupica about his father. "He never said too much about owning his own team until he had a chance to get the Cowboys," Stephen said. "Then he didn't talk about anything else for a year."

Well he's still talking. And, these days, there's plenty to say.

TAKING THE

On Saturday, February 25, 1989, *The Dallas Morning News* was probably the only paper in the country not to lead with an account of an airplane disaster that swept nine passengers to their deaths over the Pacific Ocean. But Dallas was facing a disaster of its own.

Word had it that the Dallas Cowboys were about to be sold. To a millionaire from Arkansas, no less.

That story got top billing.

The sale was not a total surprise, however. Owner Bum Bright had had the Cowboys on the block for 11 months, following a three-year decline that included the team's first losing season in two decades in 1986, and a worst-in-the-league 3-13 record in 1988.

Cowboy head coach Tom Landry remained in his office. Working. While the phones rang off the hook, inquiring about the new owner, the old coach, and the fate of the Cowboys themselves. Then he left for his vacation home at Lakeway, outside Austin.

The official word came the next day:

Landry was out.

New owner Jerry Jones was indeed an Arkansas oil millionaire.

And the new coach was Jimmy Johnson, Jones's college roommate and teammate on the unbeaten 1964 University of Arkansas

Razorback football team. Currently coach at the University of Miami. Owner of a 52-9 record. And the 1987 national NCAA championship.

Tom Landry had compiled a sterling record in his tenure with the Cowboys. His 250 wins, 162 losses and 6 ties placed him third on NFL's all-time victory list. His teams won 13 division championships, five NFC titles and two Super Bowls. And he set an NFL record with 20 consecutive winning seasons (1966-1985). Hired when the Cowboys were formed in 1960 and the only coach the team had ever known, Landry tied with former Green Bay coach Curly Lambeau for consecutive seasons coaching the same team—29.

But the glory days were gone. And changes were coming fast. Jones and Cowboys president Tex Schramm flew to Lakeway over the weekend to give the news to Landry as he was stepping off the golf course. Within two months, Schramm himself would be gone, as would others in the organization.

Landry, the one most slighted, would say only, "It could have been handled better." Typically a gentleman, he said later, "It wouldn't be fair to keep me around hanging over everybody's shoulder."

Explaining the need "to go in another direction," Jones said, "It was not an easy decision."

REINS: 1989

Michael Irvin: "I feed off the challenge."

Jones immediately announced positive intentions. "We must win. We will win. Winning is the name of the game," he said. "We're going to win this year."

But if the participants were resigned to their fates, the players, sportswriters and fans were not so sure. Jones received two death threats. And bumper stickers around Dallas read "Money can't buy class, Mister Jones."

Said Herschel Walker: "It's sad. The saddest thing is to see someone go not knowing what in the world's going on. For that to happen, with him not knowing...That's tough."

Randy Galloway of *The Dallas Morning News* thundered, "Common decency was violated. Get out of town, Jimmy. Give the man a decent burial, OK. He is only one of the best who ever was."

And in Austin, a reader wrote to the American Statesman, "All of those people who have taken pride in calling America's Team their own have been stabbed in the back by the Arkansas fraternity of Jones and Johnson...I for one, for the first time in 19 years, will never bother to watch another Dallas Cowboys football game."

The 45-year-old Johnson was not at the press conference announcing the sale. But Landry's firing put him in a terribly difficult position. When he faced the press for the first time a few days later, the first question asked was, "Because of the way things were handled, you and Jerry Jones are not the most popular people in town right now. How do you respond to that?"

Meanwhile, in April, the City of Dallas held Tom Landry Appreciation Day, and 50,000 people packed City Hall Plaza to show their appreciation and affection for the deposed coach.

Johnson didn't inherit much when he arrived in Dallas. Herschel Walker, a 27-year-old running back acquired only recently, was the team's leading producer, a two-time Pro Bowl participant who had gained more than 91 percent of the entire backfield's rushing total the previous year. Michael Irvin, the team's number-one draft choice the year before, was injured.

But there was a bright spot. The Cowboys' sorry showing the previous year had earned them the number-one draft choice for 1989. Dallas had not landed a spectacular high-round draftee since acquiring Tony Dorsett in 1977. This year, Johnson picked UCLA quarterback Troy Aikman, signed him to a six-year $11.037-million contract and handed him jersey number 8. The new coach didn't do badly with his other picks, either. Number two was Daryl Johnston, a Syracuse fullback, and number three was Mark Stepnoski, a Pittsburgh guard who would become the Cowboys' center.

In the supplemental draft, Johnson brought on board University of Miami quarterback Steve Walsh, who passed up his senior year to play professionally for his old coach.

In 1989 Tony Tolbert became the first rookie to start at defensive end for the Cowboys since Randy White in 1975.

After Ken Norton Jr.'s rookie year he was labeled a "disappointment" by a national magazine. Not!

In all, that first draft netted 14 new Cowboys (plus Walsh). Johnson said he was looking mostly for players who would help the team right away and players who would improve the defensive line. "For the most part," he said, "these players are overachievers. They are tough players. Contact players who don't mind hard work and who enjoy competition. Players who like to mix it up."

Players, in other words, like he had been.

The first year was tough. "Everything was in total disarray," said veteran Bill Bates. Jimmy Johnson put it another way: "I've got respect for Tom Landry and his coaching staff. And they were last in the league the year before. So I think that tells you what kind of talent was here when I got here."

Troy Aikman made a good showing in training camp. "I like what everyone else likes—his strong arm," said Cowboys cornerback Everson Walls. But he withheld final judgment, noting

that "passing drills are like target practice...You have to wait and get in pads and see how he reads defenses, handles the rush."

Wide receiver Kelvin Martin, out of Boston College, also was wary, seeming to know what lay in store: "You have to go through the bad times before you can experience the good times." And in that first season of the Johnson-Jones regime, the bad times were very bad indeed.

First came Johnson's revolving door.

When training camp opened in July at Cal-Lutheran University in Thousand Oaks, California, Johnson declared, "I want the most talented player on the field, regardless of experience. The best players will play." The emphasis was definitely on youth, prompting one sportswriter to tag them the Clearasil Cowboys.

The players liked the idea. At first. Said defensive end Tony Tolbert, a fourth-round draft pick out of UT-El Paso: "I think the

A Yankee out of Syracuse University, Daryl Johnston grew up just outside of... Buffalo.

them—appeared during the regular season. There was so much turnover over the next few seasons that by the time the Cowboys made the Super Bowl in 1993, only 16 players from Johnson's first team remained on the roster.

"The team picture was a classic," defensive coordinator Dave Wannstedt recalled. "There was just an influx of guys who just happened to be there that week for the picture. There were guys in the picture nobody knew, because they weren't there the next week."

Then the horrible season itself. After a promising 2 and 1 preseason, the Cowboys won only one and lost 15 games that year. In the opener, New Orleans humiliated the Cowboys on national television 28-0—only the third regular-season blanking in team history. Dallas went scoreless in losses to New York and Philadelphia, too. The Cowboys's average points per game were 12.75, a new team low. Other new team records included: Fewest first downs (seven) and fewest total yards (108) in a game, and most first downs in a season by opponents (321). Dallas tied the NFL record for the most losses in a season (15, shared with New Orleans, who had their bad year in 1980). The Cowboys didn't score a touchdown in the final nine quarters of the season.

The bad times did make for some good jokes, however. Lots of them. For example: "A woman drops her three kids off at a Cowboys game. Later, someone from the stadium calls her: 'Ma'am, could you come get your kids? They're beating the Cowboys 14-3.'" Then there was the fax going around various Dallas offices about the Cowboys 1989 schedule, listing Irving Junior High School, Cub Scout Pack 101 and the Texas Blind Academy as opponents.

Green Bay, another team on the ropes, was saying hopefully: "Hey we get to play Dallas twice."

The team's only high point occurred November 5, when the 14.5-point underdog Cowboys beat the Washington Redskins 13-3. With Aikman sidelined with a broken finger, Steve Walsh led the

team at quarterback. The secondary made two interceptions. Walsh handed off to running back Paul Palmer for two key plays, a 47-yard scamper to the six, and a two-yard touchdown dive that gave the Cowboys the lead. Palmer rushed for his first 100-yard game in the victory that day. But he, too, was a victim of the revolving door.

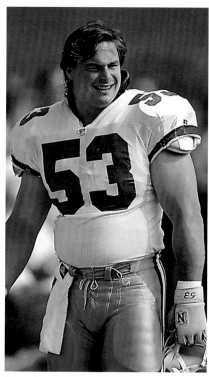

A two-time Academic All-American at Pittsburgh, Mark Stepnoski has started 55 consecutive games at center for the Cowboys.

young guys are glad to be coming into a situation where they'll get a real chance to play."

The constant search for the best players—and it lasted all season—bred uncertainty, however. Looking back on that first season four years later, Bates recalled, "The first year it was like, 'Who's he going to cut today? Who's starting this week? Do I still have a job?'"

As it turned out, just about everyone and his grandmother had a job. Briefly. Johnson rotated players in and out of practice and games at terrific speed. More than half the 47-man team had not been Cowboys in 1988, and 64 players—41 different starters among

After graduating from the Air Force Academy, Chad Hennings, like Roger Staubach before him, served four years in military service, including flying in the Gulf War, before joining the Cowboys.

By the season-ending game against Green Bay, he didn't even suit up.

It was Johnson's first victory since the Orange Bowl game 10 months earlier. "We're going to have a lot of wins over the next so-many years in Dallas, and it's good to get it started," he crowed.

"O-fer is over" trumpeted *The Dallas Morning News*. But there would be no more wins that year.

The real legacy of 1989, however, was not in the games lost, but in an event that occurred in the middle of the season. When Johnson shocked fans with another announcement almost as big as Landry's dismissal.

He had traded Herschel Walker to the Minnesota Vikings.

In the deal, Dallas received five players, Minnesota's 1992 number-one draft pick and six conditional picks. Immediately, Dallas took from Minnesota cornerback Issiac

Holt, linebackers Jesse Solomon and David Howard, running back Darrin Nelson and defensive end Alex Stewart. The blockbuster swap eventually brought Emmitt Smith and Russell Maryland, among others. It also, according to Jones, did something else: It gave fans, players and coaches hope. And a future.

Johnson called the trade, "probably the most positive thing that happened this year." Explained Jones, "The fundamentals of this trade were the draft picks for the future of the Dallas Cowboys."

The wisdom of trading a star like Walker was elusive. (Certainly it eluded Minneapolis.) As Troy Aikman told *Sport* magazine: "The way I saw it, just as a rookie, how can you trade a Herschel Walker? He was the only established player we had, offensively. The one guy we had to look to. But I can see it from Coach Johnson's view too."

Walker had been among the league leaders in total offense the year before, and the team had won only three games."

The Walker trade, in fact, was based on the following premise: You can't build a team starting with a great running back because running backs don't last very-long—only 3.1 years on the aver-age. Johnson wisely recognized that by the time the team had "caught up" with Walker, the star would be in decline. So he traded Walker, built the team up and picked running backs—namely Emmitt Smith—when the team was ready.

By the end of 1989, it seemed obvious that, like the Walker trade, there was more behind Johnson's changes than met the eye. It may have been fate. In late November, when the Cowboys were 1-11, *The Dallas Morning News* ran a story explaining that teams at the end of three decades—the 1959 Green Bay Packers, the 1969 Pittsburgh Steelers, the 1979 San Francisco 49ers—all had racked up horrible seasons with new coaches but had gone on to greatness. Could the Cowboys be part of this trend?

It's also worth noting that Tom Landry's first team went 0-11-1, that the fewest points the Cowboys ever scored in a season was 177 in 1960, and that few games of the 1-15 season were real blowouts. The worst Cowboy defeat ever did not come during this year. That had been a 44-point loss (44-0) to Chicago in 1985. The second worst defeat was by 41 points (48-7), against Cleveland in 1960.

In the end, even those who had a vision for the future had mixed feelings about 1989. "It really was a season just to feel out things," Johnson said, as it ended. "If our goal had been to make the playoffs, we wouldn't have been bringing in three or four players each week. If our plan was to make the playoffs, we wouldn't have traded Herschel Walker."

Four years later, as the Cowboys were about to enter the Super Bowl, Johnson said he knew he'd "turn it around." But he also noted: "It was the most miserable year of my life."

JIMMY JOHNSON:
RETURN OF A NATIVE SON

★ ★ ★ ★

"I did not know for sure what I was doing," Jimmy Johnson said upon being hired. "But I did not doubt myself."

James William Johnson is a natural coach. Born forty-nine years ago in Port Arthur, Texas, the son of C.W. and Allene Johnson, he was driven to succeed early on. "We would always tell him what a good game he played and how proud we were," his mother recalls. But he always said, 'I could have done better.'

Sounds just like a coach. Sure, he had plenty of intelligence and innate ability, but his outstanding characteristic was his extraordinary willpower.

Port Arthur is a Gulf Coast oil refinery town—Fina, Texaco, Chevron—and has known plenty of hard times. The town's favorite son had local area competition in the luminary department: Tex Ritter, the Big Bopper, Bum Phillips and Johnson's classmate Janis Joplin, with whom he went to high school in 1960 and '61.

James William Johnson's football rise began for a local football power, the Jefferson High Yellowjackets, where he earned All-State honors as an undersized linebacker and defensive lineman. A teammate called him "the best player I ever saw and you could tell it would take him a long way." No question there.

His football ferocity earned him a full scholarship to the University of Arkansas. There, he was a teammate of a young man named Jerry Jones, who was team captain, of the Razorbacks' unbeaten 1964 team that ended up tied with Notre Dame and Joe Willie Namath's Alabama team for the national championship.

When the NFL ignored Johnson, the diminutive All-Southwest Conference defensive lineman went looking for work. Football work. His first job came at Louisiana Tech—$1,000 a month, which sounds amusing now, but was respectable then. The attraction was immediate. "It was like bridge, only better," Johnson says. "There were X's and O's strategy, but it wasn't only that. It was rewarding to me to take players who weren't as good as the other team's and win."

All coaches are motivators. "Treat a person as if he were what he could be and should be and he will become what he could be and should be," Johnson says. Straight out of "What They Don't Teach You at Harvard Business School," which adorned Johnson's desk when he coached at Miami.

The coaching phenom moved up quickly, a habit that would continue—from Wichita State to Iowa State to Oklahoma and back to Arkansas, where he was defensive line coach under Frank Broyles. At the same time he was developing his own philosophy of life and football. "I don't like b.s." he has said. Mentors like Broyles and Chuck Fairbanks, both no-nonsense types, would doubtless approve. "I'm a perfectionist. I am intense. I like things a certain way. I'm uncomfortable when they're not right."

Johnson moved to an outstanding University of Pittsburgh team as assistant head coach and defensive coordinator for two years before getting his first head-coaching position at Oklahoma State. In his first season there he was named Big Eight Coach of the Year, and in five years had a 29-25 record with two bowl trips. Then the University of Miami called. And Jimmy Johnson, a man who had done 14 long years as an assistant college coach before grabbing

a head job, who was by no means a "star," began a remarkable roll to coaching stardom.

Miami was not just successful, it was triumphant. Beginning in 1984 Johnson led his Hurricanes to a 52-9 record in five seasons and took them to the national championship in 1987. Some statistics: A 36-game consecutive winning streak, the fifth longest in NCAA history; a 20-game road winning skein; a 21-9 record against teams ranked in the Top 20.

Then the telephone rang and Jimmy Johnson was going home

Johnson emphasized the "team" concept early and often.

A college psychology degree can come in handy while dealing with referees.

to Texas. But there was a hitch. A big one. He was replacing Tom Landry. The legend. Who had been canned by Jerry Jones, Johnson's old Razorback teammate, approximately four nanoseconds after he'd bought the franchise. History hasn't recorded whether Johnson gulped, but the response would have been appropriate.

The Landry firing put the 45-year old Johnson in a tough spot . He is a man familiar with controversy. "It seems every job I take, I take some crap. I got to Oklahoma State and they were on probation and being investigated for some other violations. I go to Miami and they say, 'Who is this hick from Oklahoma?' I come here and they say, 'What's this college boy doing coaching the Cowboys?'"

Sometimes you can't win for losing. But according to Johnson it was actually easier to begin in Dallas than Miami, where he inherited a national championship team. "Everybody [in Dallas] knew it was rock bottom. So they were more receptive to any kind of success." And, at least, Johnson was a Texan who had grown up a Cowboy fan.

Not that his leaving Miami was adversarial. When the Dallas rumors first surfaced, Miami's athletic director said, "If he does decide to go, it would be an impressive step forward and we wish him well. I thank him for the great things he has done for the University of Miami."

Johnson is an unusual package as a man. At first glance he might seem a stereotypical old-fashioned, hard-rock coach. And he is that, but he's also much more. Dallas sportswriter Ed Werder describes

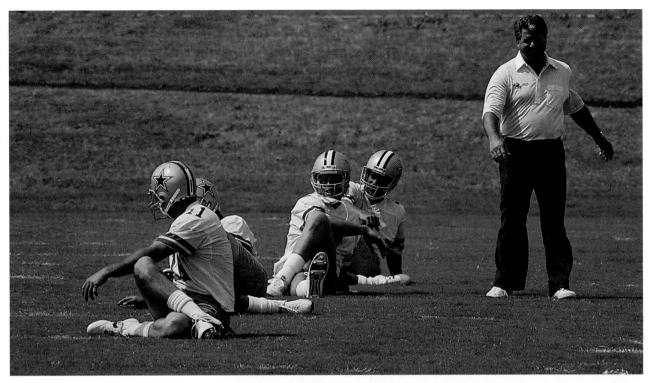

Johnson as "a little unpredictable," pointing out that the coach majored in psychology and is more than a little adept at motivating his players. Most stereotypes don't major in psychology. On the other hand, few psychology types say things like, "Nobody really knows me completely. And that's the way I like it."

But he is also, by many accounts, a wonderful friend. New Chicago Bears head coach and long-time protege Dave Wannstedt says, "There is no person in my life who has influenced me more than Jimmy Johnson."

With success come accolades. And, in the NFL, job offers. So it was with Dallas' resident defensive genius, Dave Wannstedt, grabbed by the Chicago Bears after the NFC Championship game to replace Mike Ditka. Like his friend Jimmy Johnson before him, Wannstedt would be succeeding a legend.

The Bears' pursuit of Wannstedt was not a lonely one. He had previously turned down the University of Pittsburgh, his alma mater, and other college job offers. (Wannstedt has a historical Cowboy connection; ironically, the defensive whiz was an offensive tackle at Pitt,

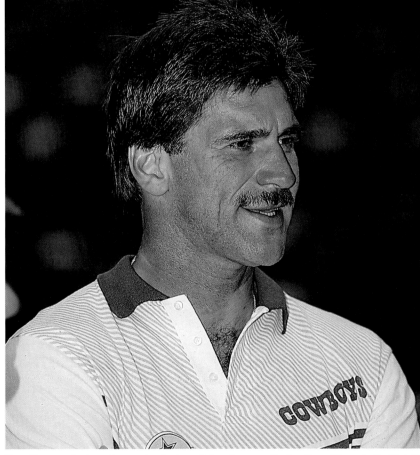

Sometimes, winning also means losing. Defensive coordinator Dave Wannstedt officially became the Chicago Bear coach February 1, 1993, the day after the Super Bowl victory.

28

where he blocked for Tony Dorsett.) Then the Giants came calling. And Wannstedt in New York would have been tough on Johnson. His friend in the same division? "Our relationship would have probably deteriorated if he remained in this division," Johnson admits candidly. "He understands me better than most people, better sometimes than I know myself, and I knew our relationship would be better if he was with the Bears."

Their relationship has been a long one. Wannstedt worked with Johnson at Pitt, followed him to Oklahoma State, and eventually rejoined him in 1986 as defensive coordinator for the Miami Hurricanes. Wannstedt had been coaching the Miami Dolphins' linebackers for a month when Jimmy Johnson was made Cowboy coach and the phone rang once again.

In his four seasons, Wannstedt's defensive unit improved from 20th-ranked in 1989 (347.3 yards per game) to the top-ranked spot in '92 (245.8). Johnson gave Wannstedt, 40, his blessing to take the job at Chicago. And in a characteristically unusual move allowed the negotiation and announcement to occur before the Super Bowl—making the Cowboys defensive coach a lame duck during the two most important weeks of the football. "I felt it would happen and he deserved it," Johnson said. "I didn't want to keep him from a top job by making him wait until after the Super Bowl. When he relayed to me which way he wanted to go, I decided we should get it done prior to the Super Bowl."

Most of all Jimmy Johnson is a driven man.

He is a self-admitted workaholic. "I'm about winning," he says. That makes him a perfect match for Cowboy owner Jerry Jones. According to former NFL coach Ron Meyer, the relationship between Jones and Johnson "is the best in the NFL. They both know football, and they both know business."

"I don't think I ever could have the responsibility with other teams that I have here," Johnson says. There was good reason for the trust, according to Jones: "He has a combination of intellect and people skills that you don't see very often."

"The man thrives on being the best," says Emmitt Smith.

A lot was made during Super Bowl week of the fact that Johnson could be the first coach to win a national collegiate championship and an NFL championship. His football philosophy has been the same at both levels. First get a top-flight, star quarterback, then a superior defensive line, and go from there. "That's something I've done everywhere I've been," Johnson says. "I believe you have to be dominant in those two areas first."

The coach always sends a clear message to his players: "If you're really committed to being the very best, you have to put in the time." Troy Aikman says it's a two-way street: "He's a very competitive person, a very driven person."

Johnson's never lacked for confidence. On his arrival in Dallas he said, "We're going to be in the Super Bowl." The image he sends to players is crystal clear. "I want them to see someone who's going to win day in and day out. Year in and year out." And he knows how he wants to get there. Michael Irvin describes the methodology: "This is the way I'm going to do it. If you don't like it...c'est la vie." "The way" means "my way." Frank Sinatra would approve.

Johnson is so consumed with the game that he can fairly be described as reclusive; a private man in a public job. That doesn't stop people from talking about him. Speculating about him.

Take for example, his now-famous perfectly coiffed hair. Why the pomade? Johnson's not the type of man to dodge a question. On the other, a full explanation can't be counted on. Yes, he uses something on it. But he doesn't explain why.

His father, C.W., fessed up to the *Houston Chronicle:* "His hair is like mine. If you don't put something on it, we look like [boxing promoter] Don King."

Even Jimmy Johnson can't control everything. But what he does, he controls brilliantly.

BUILDING A CHAMPION: 1990

"IT'S NOT WHETHER WE WILL SUCCEED. WE WILL. IT'S JUST A MATTER OF HOW LONG IT WILL TAKE."
—JIMMY JOHNSON, (1990)

By 1992 Jay Novacek had become the first Cowboy tight end to catch 50 passes in three consecutive seasons.

When the Cowboys got together for camp in July of 1990, it must have seemed like it took the better part of the first week just to say hello. Forty-eight new players looking for a spot on opening day. Forty-eight guys who were more than willing to fight for a job. The revolving door seemed to have been invented for Jimmy Johnson and his staff. The only thing tougher must have been the "if you don't like the weather, just wait a second" climate of Texas in mid-summer. Cool and rainy one day, hot as hell the next. Johnson, whose iron will had been forged in the blast furnace that passes for weather in the southern tip of Florida, even rejected the offer of a tent to protect his players from the blazing sun. "I don't want players to think of shade when there's work to do," he declared.

And there was a lot of work to be done. In '89, 1 and 15 hadn't done much to encourage the hopeful, and Johnson promised a wide-open camp with no guarantees for anyone. The pressure was on. Jerry Jones kept the game ball from the previous year's single victory in his office. His explanation: "I had a friend that came by after last season and said, 'You know Jerry, you're the only owner in the NFL that can say that's my win.' Yep, that was it last year." The owner was philosophical, with just a touch of cayenne about 1989. "If I let all the dry holes in my life get me down, I'd never have done anything. You've just

got to be tolerant of failure," he said. Certainly there was plenty to be tolerant of that first year.

The new, aggressive, risk-taking approach that would increasingly be seen on the field also began to be felt in the front office. Director of player personnel Bob Ackles said in 1990, "Before [Johnson/Jones], there was always a concern about getting screwed in a deal. So we didn't make them. In 1987, we traded with the Seahawks for a tackle, Ron Essink. We gave them a fifth-round choice and Essink retired on us almost immediately. After that, we were just too careful."

That wasn't the case anymore. The Dallas office complex, which for years had been a symbol of uptight corporate style football, was beginning to resemble a wide-open Texas cattle town. Deals were being made. Twenty-five in 22 months. Some good, some not. The two biggest, however, Walker to the Vikings and Walsh soon to go, netted eight picks out of the first three rounds in '90, '91, and '92, plus some quality players. Things were happening. It was fun to work for the Cowboys again.

Johnson had worked the team hard, and while some of the players might have grumbled about how hard, they were in top condition. The veterans might have questioned Johnson's "rah-rah" motivational techniques, but there was a feeling at the end of training camp...not so much about whether this would be the year, but that for the first time in a long

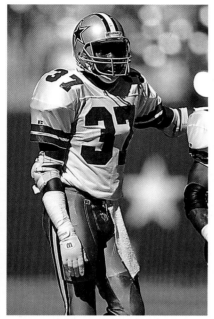

A plan B signing from the Rams, James Washington was a bargain.

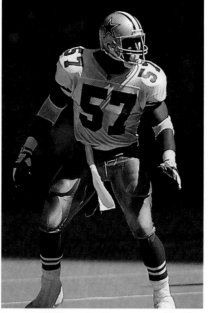

Free agent Vinson Smith was a steal for the Cowboys.

Kenneth Gant made "The Shark" the latest dance craze.

time things were going in the right direction. For Johnson it wasn't a question of IF...it was a question of WHEN.

The 1990 season began on a strong note. The decision to trade Walsh had been made, and Aikman was in the driver's seat. Toughened by a grueling conditioning regime and a demanding coach, the Cowboys came back in the fourth quarter to defeat the San Diego Chargers 17-14 in their first game. Said Johnson, "These guys have worked hard. We had a tough camp, and they have done

everything possible to get ready for the opening game. I think the effort was outstanding."

The Cowboys outscored the Chargers 10-0 in the fourth and rolled up 96 of their 249 yards. "We feel the fourth quarter is ours, and we're going to be stronger than any team we play in the fourth quarter because we work at it," said defensive end Jim Jeffcoat. "Jimmy works us hard, but he works us hard to win."

Hard work, dedication and enthusiasm weren't enough to insure victory in the next three

games, however. The Cowboys were blown out twice by the Giant juggernaut and they lost a close one to the Redskins. But running back Emmitt Smith's first full game turned some Washington heads. "Awesome—there's just one word to describe him," Washington defensive end Fred Stokes said. Dallas squeaked by Tampa in game four but got trashed by Phoenix the following week. The coaches and staff looked at it all as a learning experience. They had gone into the season expecting more wide-

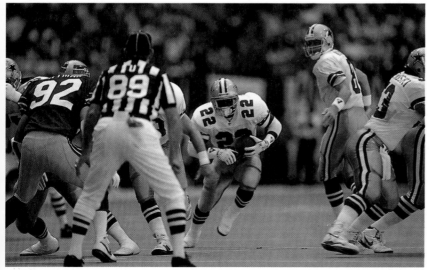

"I've never seen a running back like him," Troy Aikman says of Emmitt Smith.

"I don't want players to think of shade when there's work to do"
–Jimmy Johnson

"If you don't like it, c'est la vie."
–Michael Irvin

open, run-and-shoot offenses along the lines of the Falcons and Oilers. What they were seeing was something else. "It's like the football Vince Lombardi taught," said John Wooten, Cowboy pro personnel director. "Teams have turned back the clock. It's almost like football has gotten back to being a pride thing. Teams come out and say, 'We're going to kick your butt.' They're playing hard-nosed, in-your-face football and trying to dominate games physically."

Evidently Tampa hadn't yet heard, because the Cowboys bush-whacked them a second time and then had a week to feel good before they lost a squeaker to the Eagles, 21-20. "This one has probably turned into a bigger rivalry for us than Washington and the Giants," said quarterback Troy Aikman said. By the end of week 10, the Cowboys were 3 and 7. The fans were wondering, and the coaches might have been, too. But the young team was beginning to learn about how to be winners. "Troy stays calm under adverse conditions," linebacker Jack Del Rio said. "He's not a guy that gets rattled...The feeling is 'Let's hang in there, stay with it and things will fall into place.'" And how. The Cowboys rebounded to win

At the University of Miami Jimmie Jones teamed with Russell Maryland and Cortez Kennedy to form one the finest defensive lines in college history.

four in a row and move into play-off contention in December. But after Aikman suffered a separat-ed shoulder, the Cowboys lost their final two games for a 7-9 fin-ish.

After finishing with the NFL's worst record at 1-15 in Johnson's first year, the Cowboys went down to the final seconds of their final regular season game before being eliminated from playoff contention by Atlanta.

All in all it was a spectacular effort, and a satisfying season. The Cowboys had played with courage and toughness. And emo-tion. Johnson, one of his shrewder players observed, knew that his

"Jimmy works us hard, but he works us hard to win."
–Jim Jeffcoat

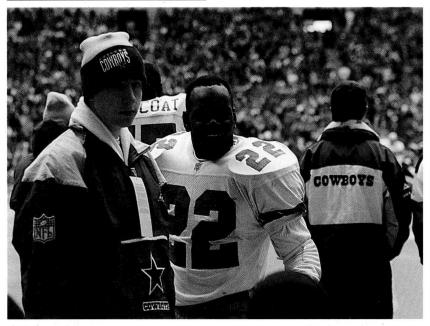

"As Emmitt Smith goes," says the Eagles' Wes Hopkins, "so go the Cowboys."

players would have to win on emotion until the talent caught up. The price of poker in Dallas was going up, and anyone that came to play would need a pretty large bankroll.

"When I came here we were slightly above zero, Johnson said, "I think we're in the middle of the pack right now." Not yet where they wanted to be but one step closer to the brass ring, and a lot of veterans were hoping they'd be around when it was time to grab it. If you believed Jimmy Johnson and Jerry Jones, they wouldn't have to wait long...not very long at all. As Jones said at the beginning of the season, "The Dallas Cowboys should be in the playoffs. That's just something that has been a given in NFL history and that's what I expect."

It hadn't happened in 1990, and the pundits were saying the Cowboys were still a year or more away. But late in the season, after Dallas had whipped Phoenix by 31 points, Jones raised his glass in the owner's box and laughed, saying, "This is what we thought it'd be like when we bought the team."

His coach raised his glass in response. "And there's more to come."

Players who look like movie stars don't usually make The All-Madden Team. Aikman did in 1991.

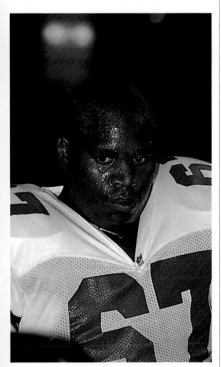

No. 1 draft choice Russell Maryland.

TROY AIKMAN: YOUNG GUN RISING

The quarterback as heartthrob, kid-lover and fantasy date.

Within weeks of his appointment as Cowboys head coach, Jimmy Johnson flew to California to watch Troy Aikman work out with the UCLA Bruins...and came back with his mind made up: "We knew without question Troy Aikman was our guy when we got back on the plane."

And when the Cowboys and 22-year-old Aikman formally struck their deal, there was no doubt how much they wanted him, either. $11.037 million worth, more than any other rookie in NFL history and third among all players active at the time. And on an annual basis, more than the Cowboys' own, much-sought after running back, Herschel Walker. Aikmania had arrived.

Was he worth it? "It's a lot of money for a guy who hasn't taken a snap," said New York Giants general manager George Young. But the Cowboys organization wasn't worried. Said Johnson, "Troy has the talent to take the Cowboys back to where we all want them to be."

As for Aikman, he was exactly where he wanted to be. Dallas, Texas. "It's pretty much a dream come true for me," he said. "It's beyond words. I wanted this so badly, to be a Dallas Cowboy."

That dream began back in Henryetta, Oklahoma, a town of 6,000, about 200 miles north of Dallas, where his parents had moved (from California) when he was 12, and where, as a high school student, he earned All-State honors as a member of the Henryetta Fighting Hens football team...and where he was a Cowboys fanatic. In his words: "It seemed like every Sunday the Dallas Cowboys were on TV, and Roger Staubach was throwing the last minute touchdown pass to win the ballgame."

Aikman enrolled in the University of Oklahoma, but transferred to UCLA after two years. Redshirted for a year, he led the Bruins to a 20-4 record his remaining two years (including the 1988 Aloha Bowl and 1989 Cotton Bowl wins) and was named All American. He completed 64.8 percent of his passes for 5,298 yards and 41 touchdowns. He was ranked the third-best-passer in NCAA history.

Then Johnson came calling. And Aikman went to work. Because under Johnson, whose mission was to create a new—and winning—Cowboy team, even Aikman wasn't assured of a job. "There's not a starting player on the team," the coach said. "They have to earn it."

Aikman was the only rookie to work out with the veterans in a three-day mini-camp that spring. And he wasn't expecting to start. "There's a lot of competition, and I understand that," he said. "And it's going to be some time before I'm ready to go and really compete for the position. The timetable hasn't been set. But hopefully, I'll be there in a relatively short period."

"A dream come true." –Troy Aikman

But in Aikman's case, relative meant very short. The Cowboys had three quarterbacks, all of whom were either aging, injured, inexperienced or error-prone. And the team and the fans needed Aikman. He became the first rookie since Roger Staubach in 1969 to start a season opener for Dallas.

Staubach. That name would do more than inspire Aikman, the Henryetta Fighting Hen. It would haunt Aikman, the Cowboy. Because when you're a fabulously well-paid star like Aikman, everyone expects you to match the legendary feats of past heroes. And comparisons flow freely.

After his debut in a preseason game against Denver (which the Cowboys lost, 24-21), Aikman was not only compared to Broncos' quarterback John Elway, but to his predecessors. Fortunately, the notices were favorable. Noted The Denver Post: "Troy Aikman inherits the shoes once worn by Roger Staubach, Don Meredith and Danny White (providing he can win the job from fellow freshman Steve Walsh). Someday, Aikman could be another Elway. If he stays healthy, Aikman may have a run at greatness."

The comparisons stayed with him. On the eve of the Super Bowl more than four years later, after the Cowboys had whipped the entire State of Texas into a Cowboy-loving frenzy, he still couldn't shake Staubach's ghost. "The legend of Roger Staubach will always dance just out of Aikman's grasp," wrote the *Fort Worth Star Telegram* during Super Bowl Week. "He forever will be measured by the Staubach standard," wrote Randy Galloway, sports columnist for *The Dallas Morning News*. "Such an unfair burden, yes. But if you can't live with it, you can't live here. Only one thing to do. If there's a winnable game, go win it."

Unfortunately, in that first year, there were few winnable games. And Aikman didn't stay healthy.

Aikman missed five games with a broken left index finger. He didn't even play in the Cowboys single victory that miserable first year.

There were some bright spots. Aikman threw for 379 yards—a NFL rookie record—in the Cowboys' 24-20 loss to Phoenix. He threw 56 passes without an interception and led the team in rushing toward the end of the season. He was named to most All-Rookie teams. But he threw four interceptions in the season-ending game against Green Bay. And he was disappointed that Herschel Walker had been sent packing. At the end of the season, he informed his agent he hoped also to be traded.

"There is no way I ever envisioned it would be the way it is right now," he told *Sport* magazine. "I couldn't imagine the Dallas Cowboys ever being as bad as we've been."

As much as he wanted to win, however, Aikman had other priorities. "Frankly," he continued, "it was more important for me to be happy where I was living. The environment, the atmosphere, those kind of things mean a lot to me. I like where I came from. I wanted more of that."

Cool in the pocket.

Later, Jimmy Johnson would ascribe similar motives to his quarterback: "It's not important to Troy to go out and throw for 350 yards in a game. He just wants to win. He could throw for as many yards as he wanted to, but that's not what he's about."

What is Aikman about?

Back in 1989, Jerry Jones said, "We were not drafting just a quarterback. We were also drafting a human quality that Troy Aikman has." And that person has proved to be important to the Cowboys.

Troy Aikman is "cowboy cool." When a national advertising agency put out a report on celebrity appeal in 1992, it described him this way: "Youthful, laid-back, country-boy charm...Troy Donahue with a Southern drawl...perfect for Dr. Pepper, KFC, Copenhagen or any other product with down-home appeal."

But that image sometimes bothers Aikman. When he appeared on an Oprah Winfrey show called "Fantasy Dates," he wore boots and jeans—as he was told. But other guests wore suits. Which prompted Aikman to complain about misconceptions. He's not, he said, just an Okie who says "y'all" a lot.

> *"A lot of money for a guy who hasn't taken a snap."*
> *–George Young*

Shaping his quarterbacking place in history is one thing. You've got a level playing field. But the public's perception of his personality may already be slanted up toward a pedestal. "Let's be honest," Coach Jimmy Johnson has said. "Troy came to this city at a time it was hungry for a hero. He fit the mold beautifully. The team is struggling and along comes this good-looking, single, All-American quarterback with a bit of Southern gentleman in him. They embraced him." He's a symbol...larger than life. Cool Hand Luke.

But a cool quarterback has to be a popular quarterback with the team. "Troy has become very assertive, and his performance has commanded the respect of the players," says Johnson. "As time goes on and as we improve offensively, more and more of the players are looking to him to make things happen."

Aikman's seen it before. "I think our teams at UCLA took on my personality," he recalls. "I never was a holler-and-scream guy. There was a quiet confidence that kind of surrounded the whole offensive team. Guys never really panicked in situations. We always believed we were going to be able to come back."

Things looked pretty grim for Aikman and the Cowboys at the end of disastrous 1989. The next two years, Aikman suffered injuries (shoulder in 1990, knee in 1991) that took him out of play. Yet Aikman's own performance was aided by the improving Cowboy organization. By the time he faced the Eagles in 1991, he had been sacked by that team 20 times. The Cowboys had not scored in 11 of the 16 quarters he had played against Philadelphia. But by 1992, the Cowboy offensive line were considered among the best in the NFL. A year later, Dallas beat Philadelphia 20-10, capped by an 80-yard scoring drive led by Aikman.

As for Aikman's personal performance, the arrival of offensive coordinator Norv Turner, who added new offensive strategies and fine-tuned Aikman's technique, turned 1991 into a watershed. Aikman began the year with 93 straight passes without an interception. Then 116 more. Against Washington, he completed 27 passes for three touchdowns. And against the defending Super Bowl champion New York Giants, he threw for 84 yards in the fourth quarter and was named

NFC Offensive Player of the Week.

1992 saw even more improvements. Against Atlanta, he threw 13 straight completions. And against Denver, in a victory that clinched a playoff berth, Aikman completed 25 of 35 passes, for 231 yards and three touchdowns, including a 77-yard drive in 11

> ## "Troy Donahue with a Southern Drawl."
> ### –Ad Agency

plays. "To be able to drive the length of the field, to score and put us back ahead, that's a tremendous job by Troy Aikman and our offense," said Jimmy Johnson. But that was Aikman's job. Against San Francisco in the NFC Championship game, he threw for 322 yards.

Aikman had finally played an entire season unhurt. The Cowboys' record and his personal stats reflected it. Aikman's quarterback rating had risen from 55.7 in 1989 to 89.5 in 1992. By the time he entered the Super Bowl, Aikman was the fourth most accurate passer in NFL history, with a 60.21-percent career completion record. His performance in the playoffs boosted his rating to 116.7. For the Super Bowl itself, he earned a phenomenal 145.5. The Super Bowl, of course, saw him capture Most Valuable Player honors, completing 22 of 30 passes for 273 yards and four touchdowns.

Which just goes to validate the praise he had been getting. Said former Redskin quarterback Sonny Jurgensen, "To me, he's the next superstar in this league. Besides being tough mentally and physically, things don't bother him."

And Joe Theismann, ESPN commentator and former Washington Redskins quarterback, claimed, Troy "Troy Aikman is the next great superstar of the National Football League, if he isn't there already."

Aikman on the move.

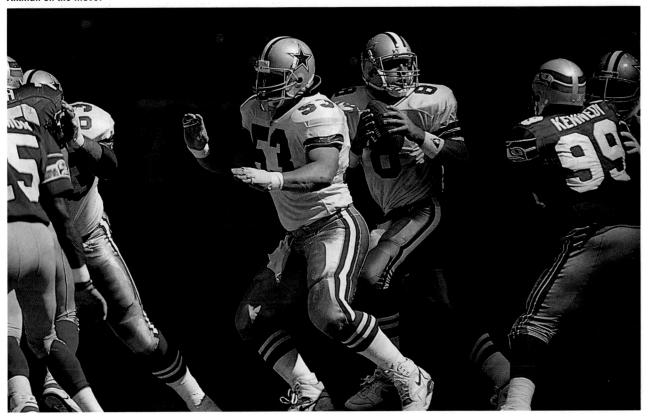

"Somewhere in the back of everyone's minds, I think, was that if the Cowboys started kicking butt, we'd feel good again. So everybody started rooting for the Cowboys subconsciously because we'd like to feel good again."
—Jerry Jones

AT LEAP FORWARD: 1991

In 1991, Texas was reeling from the recession like everyone else. Signs were everywhere and a bunch of them said "FOR SALE." Jones was right. The folks of the Lone Star State were desperate for some high times and good old-fashioned fun. They wanted their minds on something besides the hard luck which had been a steady diet since the collapse of the oil business some years back. They were ready for some magic, and Jones, like a prophet of old, like some voice crying out in the wilderness, was telling anyone who would listen that the Cowboys had some big tricks up their sleeves.

The press was less sure. Nobody doubted that the Cowboys were on their way, but the '90 season, while pretty damn good, was a long way from being solidly competitive in the NFC East, the toughest division in the NFL. Sportswriter Thomas George said in The New York Times, "Popular belief is that the Cowboys are at least two or three seasons away from Super Bowl contention, but there is little doubt that the Cowboys star is beginning to shine once again. Much of the credit has to go to Coach Jimmy Johnson—and to his understanding of players as more than meal tickets." A lot of people agreed.

Look for an 8 and 8 in '91 they all said. A solid bet for fourth place. These are growing boys...they need a little time to mature. Can't tie a steer first time you pick up a rope. Conventional wisdom said wait a while, it'll come. Problem was, Jimmy just couldn't do that. Waiting wasn't his style.

Hard work was, however, and the '91 training camp down in Austin was shaping up to be as tough as ever. 110 in the shade. The veterans, free agents, coaches and draft picks, 100 or so men, had gathered in the meeting room for the first time. Johnson started by having everyone stand, give his name, the position he played and a little something about himself. Down the line, man by man, veterans, rookies all did. Guys were cracking each other up. They were having a good old time. When it was over someone from the back of the room called out, "Hey, Coach, who are you?"

Johnson's response was quick and sharp. "I'm the guy who decides whether or not you get a paycheck every week and whether or not you have a career in this league."

Jimmy Johnson was doing what he had to do to push the

The Coach, intense and focused.

Aikman over the troops.

"Hey, Coach, who are you?"
–Anonymous Player

"They're not intimidated."
–Mark Rypien

39

team to the next step—to toughen them mentally as well as physically, because he'd seen the hype before. At Arkansas, Oklahoma State and at Miami. When a team has the scent of a winner everything changes; it's a whole new ballgame. Everybody wants something. The fans, the press, they all want a piece. That's when

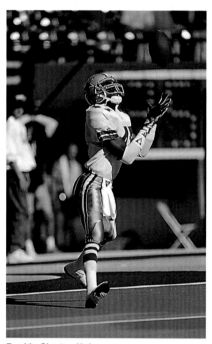

Rookie Clayton Holmes.

"Ich bin ein Beuerliner." –Rep. Dick Armey

teams get stupid. Start thinking they're immortal, that from here on everything is automatic. It was so hard to get there and so easy to let it all slide away. The press was everywhere. One of the guys said if the Cowboys hit .500 there'd be microphones in the johns. The hype went with the territory and you learned to live with it or you perished. It wasn't going to happen in Dallas. The

Cowboys were going to continue winning games in the fourth quarter because they were tough and ready, or Johnson would know the reason why.

The smell of success was in the air. Attendance was up 27% since 1988. 75,000 fans had come to watch summer camp. Both "Monday Night Football" and Turner Broadcasting's "Sunday Night Football" had received record high ratings for Cowboy games. There was even a wedding at Texas Stadium. The football flakes were back in force. Like a blast from the past, an echo from prehistoric times, something familiar was in the air—the feeling that the Cowboys were going to win. As Johnson said, "More importantly, the leaders on this team share the feeling of expecting to win. That is the most important difference in the mental and emotional makeup of the Cowboys in contrast to our team last year. Prior to the start of the '90 season, our players thought they could win. This year they fully expect to win."

They expected to have a good time as well. Weren't curfews made to be broken? After a full day of workouts and evening meetings, there was an hour before lights out to do what you darned pleased. An hour? For some guys that just wasn't enough. It was a tradition. Randy White did it. "Dandy" Don Meredith was a master of sneaking out and sneaking back. The modern generation of Cowboys were no different. "Players in the NFL call it 'going over the wall,'" said former Dallas reserve quarterback Babe Laufenberg. "I've had a lot of church socials to go to after midnight, bingo games. Church dances. I went to a Catholic school for 12 years, and I didn't want to upset the nuns."

The fines for those unfortunates who were spotted after 11:00 somewhere other than in their dorm studying pass patterns and blocking assignments were hefty. The coaches were usually less then sympathetic no matter how much imagination went into the excuse. The hand of justice was swift and firm. In 1990, only two Cowboys had been caught breaking curfew.

"They're no longer with the team," administrative assistant Bruce Mays said.

Not that there wasn't a lighter side. "One player a few years ago said he was washing his clothes," recalled Mays. "It was three in the morning, and he said he needed clean clothes for the next day. When we caught him again, he

Bold offensive coordinator Norv Turner.

"I've never enjoyed a season more." –Bill Bates

said his clothes needed to be ironed." Do the crime, you pay the fine.

If a coach sometimes had the impulse to hide a grin, he'd do it and assess the damages with a straight face. But somewhere inside he knew also that to be a winner you've got to hang loose. Managing professional athletes is a balancing act and Johnson was a master at giving and taking away. Telling the players over and over that they were ready. Saying it so many times that the saying of it made it true. They could win, would win because they were good and tough and ready. Keep that edge, because with the same certainty as death and taxes, July became August became September and the '91 season was off the drawing boards and onto the fields of play.

The great leap forward started in Cleveland on September 1, when a 17-point second quarter and 112 yards from Emmitt Smith gave the Cowboys a 26-14 win over the Browns. Dallas took the 1-0 back to Irving for a meeting with the Washington Redskins and got a little lesson in how far they still had to go. In a 33-31 squeaker the Cowboy defense wasn't quite tough enough to keep the veteran Redskins from holding on to win. The game was an old-fashioned shootout, but in the second half the Cowboys were playing without one of their top guns—Emmitt Smith had gone down with an injury. Although Dallas tacked up more total yards and more in the air, the Redskins had what counted...the win. The Cowboys, however, had delivered a message. Washington coach Joe Gibbs said, "We gradually played a little better and figured out how to slow them and get some three and outs. Everybody on the Washington side is pretty exhausted. That was a great ballgame. They're a heck of a team that has made tremendous strides. It's going to be a battle every time you play them from here on out." Gibbs, who will go down as one of the great coaches in NFL history, had, as usual, gotten it right.

The Cowboys came out of the contest bloody but not beaten. "Our goal was to win all of our home games behind this great home crowd. We can still win the rest," said Cowboy offensive guard, Kevin Gogan.

But it wasn't to be. The following week a sellout crowd of 62,656 watched in dismay as the Philadelphia Eagles buried the hapless Cowboys 24-0. Aikman was sacked a horrific 11 times. No

offense, no defense, no nuttin'. The promise of a strong season was wilting in the September Texas sun. Dallas was 1 and 2. Granted, they had lost to two of the strongest teams in the league, but the road to the Super Bowl didn't go around the good teams...it ran straight through them. It was time to get out of town, lick some wounds, and take out the frustration on Pheonix.

Dallas came on strong against the Cardinals in the first quarter with 14 points. That was enough to pull a win out of a lackluster effort by the offense, who were pretty well dominated by the Redbird defense. The Cowboys got away lucky with a 17-9 victory. But a "W" is a "W"; it doesn't matter if it's pretty or not. The Cowboys were 2 and 2 and looking down the road to the mighty Giants in Irving the following week.

Often seasons and teams and even dynasties are made on the

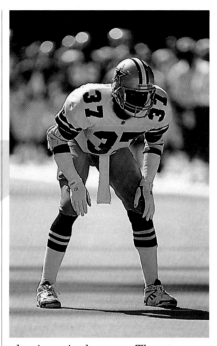

play in a single game. The Cowboys came back to Texas Stadium ready to play and play

41

they did, ambushing the Giants
with a fourth-quarter td to win, 21-
16. "This was a psychological hur-
dle we had to overcome," linebacker Jack Del Rio said. "It was
at home, it was a division game
and it was the Giants. This showed
us we can beat anybody we play.
We can now play at that level.
We're legitimate. We believe in
each other." It was a comeback
worthy of the old-time Cowboys of
Staubach and Pearson. "Roger
used to make it look so easy," Troy
Aikman said, "that the fans around
here think it is easy." Easy or not,
it was the most important win in
Aikman's and Johnson's brief
careers as Cowboys, and the
momentum and the euphoria
pushed Dallas easily past Green
Bay the following week and the
Bengals the week after. Maybe the
Cowboys would win forever.

Dallas flew up to Detroit for
week eight. They should've stayed
home. The Lions pounced, posting
24 points in the second half, and
won 34-10. Detroit just seemed to
have Dallas' number lately. Still, at
the halfway mark Dallas, to everyone's surprise, was 5 and 3 against
some pretty tough competition.

Back in Irving, the Cardinals
generated a lot of offense, but only
seven points and the Cowboys got
a breather in front of the home-
folks, 27-7. But a tough overtime
loss on the road to the Oilers pre-
ceded a thumping by the Giants in
the Meadowlands. Johnson had
strong words for the zebras after
the game on what he perceived as
a bogus defensive holding call and
generally wretched officiating.
How bad was it? "The worst since I
was four years old and my daddy
said, 'Here's what you call a football,'" was how Jimmy put it.
Suddenly a comfy 6 and 3 was 6
and 5 and the 8 and 8 preseason
predictions of the oddsmakers were
starting to look like prophecy.

Vince Lombardi is supposed to
have said, "When the going gets
tough, the tough get going."
Whether he said it or not, the
Cowboys heard it as they thundered into RFK Stadium to battle
the mighty and undefeated
Redskins. They reached deep down
inside and gutted out a game that

had it all. The contest that November 24 was a monster for the offense—399 total yards, of which Emmitt had 132 and Michael Irvin 130. The defense held off a fourth-quarter charge to topple the stunned Redskins, 24-21. And when Aikman was injured in the fourth, backup QB Steve Beuerlein, acquired at the beginning of the season from the Raiders, picked up where the starter had left off, completing 7 of 12 for 109 yards and a much-needed touchdown.

The next day, the United States House of Representatives was treated to a poetry reading by Representative Dick Armey of Lewisville, Texas, who recited an original composition to his distinguished colleagues:

A NOVEMBER POEM

"THE LOSS TOOK PLACE AT RFK
BUT EVOKES THE WORDS OF JFK.
COWBOY FANS CHANT THIS
ONELINER. SAY IT LOUD:
"ICH BIN EIN BEUERLINER"

Beuerlein had been snatched from the Raiders after volatile owner Al Davis had soured on him. The pickup was a steal for a third-round draft choice. A four-year starter at Notre Dame, Beuerlein holds virtually every passing and total offense record in the school's storied history. When Aikman went down in the years before, the Babe, Laufenberg that is, would be called upon. Beuerlein was a far better talent. "There was no panic," Emmitt Smith observed later about the reaction in the huddle to Beuerlein's entry. "Steve did a great job. He came in and led us down the field. Everybody did what they were supposed to do. We achieved our goal."

Beuerlein was typically modest: "I think I've been fortunate that Troy has been healthy for as long as he has. It's given me a chance to learn things. I wasn't sharp out there on a couple of things, but fortunately they didn't hurt us."

The implications of the victory for the near future of the Cowboys was reflected vividly in the team's reactions.

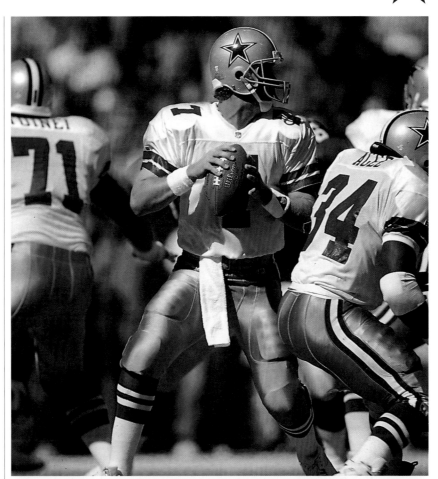

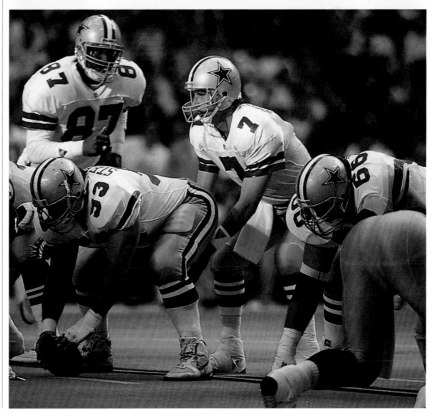

"I'm extremely proud of these guys," Coach Johnson said. "They're probably the only ones who felt that they had a shot at winning. The accolades go to the entire team. The guys were holding on with their fingernails trying to keep the Redskins out of the end zone."

"A lot of people thought we were going to get crushed," Smith said. "It really feels good to know you proved all the experts wrong." Stoical Joe Gibbs couldn't disagree: "It was kind of their day, really."

Wide receiver Alvin Harper grabbed a 34-yard touchdown catch and seemed surprised. After the game, it was almost as if the Cowboys were still pinching themselves. "They let us run freely down the field," observed Harper, "and I got real good field position on it. When I went up, I knew it was going to hit my hands and that I should come down with it. No one thought we were going to get any points out of that drive."

Washington quarterback Mark Rypien was more than a little impressed: "They're not intimidated here at all. They really play us better at RFK than in Dallas."

TV color analyst and former NFL coach, John Madden, though flamboyant in delivery, rarely over-praises anybody. After this game, he said the Cowboy victory over the Redskins involved "the greatest coaching job I've ever seen."

With this sort of praise, not to mention their own elation and satisfaction, the Cowboys were susceptible to an upset the next time. It would be a real test for the coaching staff to prepare the young team over a short week for the improving Pittsburgh Steelers. It was time to put the past in the history books and look to the future.

Aikman was still out, so the dream was in the hands of Steve Beuerlein. "A year ago," Emmitt Smith said, "the Cowboys likely would have panicked." But Beuerlein, in his first Cowboy start, had the kind of day a quarterback for a playoff-bound team is expected to have. Completing 14 of 25 passes for 217 yards, including a 66-yard bomb to Michael Irvin, Beuerlein and Dallas walked off a winner, 20-10. "It was almost like Troy was still out there," said Smith. "Steve is very good. He got in the huddle and said 'Guys, this is what we're going to do. Let's get it done.'" He even did it on a sprained ankle.

The Cowboys were 8 and 5 and headed for a grudge match at Veterans Stadium with the Philadelphia Eagles. No problem. A little holiday cheer for the fans. Dallas won it going away, 25-13. Like Santa, however, Jimmy was saving his best gift for last. On the 22nd of December 1991, Santa's mighty elves tumbled down the Falcons' chimney and stormed out the front door with all the presents in a 31-27 heartstopper. Merry Christmas, y'all. Beuerlein was Head Grinch, completing 18 passes.

For the first time since 1985 the Dallas Cowboys, runners-up to the Redskins in the NFC East, were in the playoffs. Finally, there was really something to cheer about in Dallas. The Cowboys were back and Texas had 'em.

The first round was to be played at Soldier Field, with Ditka's Bears the solid favorites. Chicago moved the ball all over the field, pushed four drives inside the Dallas 10 and reached Dallas territory seven times. Chicago could take the ball anywhere between the 20s. They just couldn't put points on the board. If you didn't have to score in football to win the game the Cowboys would have gone home, tails between their legs, and the Bears would have advanced to the next round.

But down close the developing Dallas defense just stuffed 'em. The No-Names were beginning to get some recognition. "They did a little different defense at the goal line than we had seen," said Ditka. "Things we thought could have worked did not work so well. Maybe we're a step away. Maybe we don't belong up there with the other teams. Blame me."

The Bears led in plays and yards and maintained 15 minutes

more possession time than Dallas, but it wasn't enough. Images of Doomsday flashed into fans' minds as they watched the Bears stalled time after time. "We were so keyed up we could have played five or six quarters. We knew we had to win the game defensively," said linebacker Ken Norton. The Bears were just glad it ended at four. The final was 17-13. Not an offensive gem by any stretch of the imagination, but it was good enough to send the Cowboys to Detroit and the Bears to the golf course.

Owner Jerry Jones was overwhelmed. "There's not a person in here today who doesn't believe after this game that we have a great shot at the Super Bowl. We're playing with an attitude that doesn't start five minutes before the game. It's there all week and it's constant," he glowed.

But the 1991 season ended for the Cowboys the next week, on January 5, 1992, at the Silverdome in Detroit. The Lions were inspired. Quarterback Eric Kramer had a career day, completing 29 of 38 passes for 341 yards and three touchdowns. Detroit generated 421 yards total offense and a defensive effort that yielded only two field goals. The final was a heartbreaker, 38-6. While the Lions played with intensity and power the Cowboys just couldn't seem to get off the dime. Beuerlein wasn't sharp and, even though he still wasn't 100%, Aikman replaced him late in the first half. It didn't matter. The offense just folded up and blew away.

The dream was over, but nobody was really crushed. When they took a moment to realize what had happened, the Cowboys had a lot to be proud of. "We were on a long ride, a fun ride, filled with great memories and great games. We got our hopes up. We got hopes up in Dallas. We played together, and we believed in each other. I've never enjoyed a season more." That's how Dallas veteran safety, Bill Bates summed it up.

"We had a good year," Johnson said. "Our guys did much better than anyone expected them to. But we have to become better than what we are. We will."

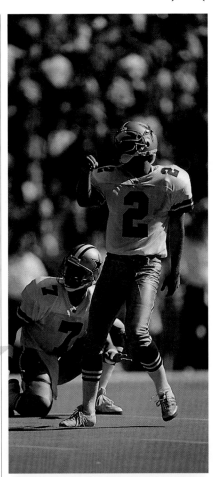

MICHAEL IRVIN:

THE PLAYMAKER

"I LOVE THE LIMELIGHT."
—MICHAEL IRVIN

It's Sunday afternoon, and here's Cowboys wide receiver Michael Irvin just where he wants to be, in front of a few thousand of his closest friends. Waving his hands to get more noise from the crowd. Spinning a towel from the sidelines to egg on the defense. Crazy about football. Crazy about the life of a football player.

"I love the limelight on Sunday afternoon," he says, "when there's 60,000 people in the stands watching me do what I've prepared to do all week."

Watching him as he pulls in pass after pass—averaging almost 18 yards per catch. Hoping for another like that 87-yard play against Phoenix last September. Quarterback Troy Aikman fires from the 13. Hits Irvin at the 22. Zoom. Past the cornerback. He's free. Down the left sideline. Touchdown!

No wonder he loves the game. His nickname is "The Playmaker." He's the one who can make it happen.

"That's what my teammates expect out of me," he has said. "When your teammates start expecting things out of you, you don't let them down. I expect to make big plays every week. That's my job."

For Michael Irvin, NFL pass-reception champ who caught six passes for 114 yards in the Super Bowl, however, the game of football and the game of life have not always produced the expected. They've been moving targets, sometimes as difficult to lay a hand on as he is.

He's known hard times: Irvin is one of 17 children. His mother was a maid. His father, a roofer and a preacher in the Primitive Baptist Church, died of cancer when Michael was in high school.

He's known good times: A member of the 1987 NCAA champion Miami Hurricanes, Irvin was drafted after his junior year with a $1.8-million contract; last summer, he signed a new $4-million deal.

He's known frustration: Irvin sat out 14 games in 1989 and 1990 with a torn anterior cruciate ligament in his right knee, a career-threatening injury.

And he's known success: He's set a slew of Cowboys records, was named Most Valuable Player in the 1991 Pro Bowl, and in 1992 ranked first in the NFL in average yardage per catch, 17.9, and second in total yards, 1,396.

He's been forced to grow up fast. "Michael," his father said the day before he died, "I feel I'm going home on the morning train, and I want you to promise to take care of your mother."

But he's sometimes had the grating cockiness of an smart-alecky kid. His first year as a Cowboy, Irvin told veteran Nate Newton that he would take the team to the Super Bowl. Later, when he found how different the NFL was from college, he returned to Newton. "Nate," he confessed, "I need help out there."

All this he freely admits, as readily as he shows his heels to an opposing player. But all the uncertainties, he says, are past. Michael Irvin has matured. As a man. As a player.

"My image now is that I'm a flamboyant player," says the 26-year-old Irvin. "My image then was that I was cocky. I was a kid then. But now I'm a man, a family man. I'm more mature."

Here's an example:

Irvin made a couple of wagers before the Super Bowl with sponsors of his local television show. One was with Kroger Food Stores. If the Cowboys lose, he said, "I'll be sacking groceries at one of Kroger's stores." The other was with Southwest Airlines. In case of a loss, he explained, "I'll be throwing luggage at Love Field." Win or lose, Kroger and Southwest would help fund trips for Dallas area youths to attend the 1993 Cowboys training camp in Austin.

Cocky? No. Flamboyant? Yes. And good-hearted, too. His father would be proud.

These are the actions of a man who loves the game which earns him his living. It's also the action of a man who has realized he must worry about his public image. "That's why I'm trying to live that [Miami] image down," he has said. "I've got sponsors. So I don't do any more crazy talking." Call it realism. Call it maturity. Whatever you call it, it's working.

Irvin's always had the drive to be a great player. At the University of Miami, he earned his degree in business management. He played football for Jimmy Johnson, setting school records for career catches (143), receiving yards (2,423) and touchdown receptions (26), and turned pro after his junior year.

When he arrived in Dallas, the first-round draft pick's attitude and talent apparently began to work again. That fall, Irvin was the first rookie receiver since Bob Hayes in 1965 to start on opening day.

But against New Orleans that first week, the man who had never missed a game because of injury bruised his ankle. He would miss four games. The inactivity was unbearable. "It was unbelievable frustration, it really was," Irvin recalled. "I left college a year early not for the money but because I didn't feel the challenge anymore. I need that challenge. I feed off that challenge."

After that season, Irvin ran off-season sprints wearing a 50-pound sandbag to increase his strength. He played racquetball and basketball. And he smarted from his image. "People say Michael is a showboat. What is a showboat?" he asked a reporter as 1989 training camp began. "Somebody who gets pumped in big games? The bigger the crowd, the more pumped I get. The more fun I have. Why am I a showboat for doing that: Why can't I just be a big game ballplayer?"

Irvin's quest to be a big-game ballplayer was sidetracked again, however, when he tore up his knee against San Francisco in October. This time he was out 364 days. This was serious.

When he returned in November 1990, the Cowboys' downfield passing game immediately came to life. "It gives our passing game some respect," said Troy Aikman, "because we can make the big plays down the field now." Said then-offensive coordinator David Shula, "We don't hesitate now to throw the ball downfield. Because

Super Bowl Touchdown!

of Michael's size and strength, he has an advantage over a lot of defensive backs. He'll outjump or outposition a defensive back for the ball. Even if he's covered, we feel the worst that can happen would be an incompletion."

The turning point came in 1991. Irvin led the league in receiving yardage (1,523). He scored eight touchdowns and had 11 catches of 25 yards or more. During the Cowboys' season-ending five-game winning streak, he caught 37 passes for 649 yards. Eleven were on third or fourth down for first downs. Four were for touchdowns. He was voted onto the first team of the 1991 Associated Press All Pro team and was named the NFL Wide Receiver of the Year. He was the first Cowboys wide receiver since Drew Pearson in 1977 to play in the Pro Bowl, where he caught eight passes for 125 yards and a touchdown and was voted Most Valuable Player.

In 1992, Irvin missed training camp due to salary negotiations—but when the season started, he was instrumental in the Cowboys' early-season winning streak. There had been some grumbling from coaches that he was "rusty." But in game three against Phoenix, Irvin caught eight passes for 210 yards and scored three touchdowns. "I don't want to hear any more about rust," he said.

By the end of the season, Irvin had been named to the Pro Bowl for the second year in a row. Over 1991 and 1992, his two complete seasons, he had caught the football 171 times for 2,919 yards. The difficult times were over.

And after a six-catch, 86-yard afternoon in which the Cowboys beat San Francisco 30-20 to win the NFC title, Irvin announced: "One more win and the big man upstairs can call me home. I've served my purpose here."

After his two-touchdown performance in the Super Bowl, Cowboy fans hope that Michael has not completely served his purpose.

EMMITT SMITH

L ate-night talk-show host Arsenio Hall tossed Emmitt Smith a football and asked, "You're very comfortable with that thing in your hand, huh?"

To which Smith grinned and replied: "Oh, very much. Very very much."

It was an answer he could have applied to any number of questions. Questions about how comfortable he feels in the spotlight at such a young age. (He's 23.) Or questions about how comfortable he is with the direction of his life. (Smith told Hall that as a high-school senior he sat in the stands at a Super Bowl game and told himself, "One day, I'm going to be right there.")

It's also an answer that a less polite player might have given about his role in the Cowboys' success.

But not Smith. "This is far from a one-man team," Smith told the *Austin American Statesman* a few days before he appeared on Arsenio. "Don't say that I'm the rushing leader who took his team to the Super Bowl. This is a team, and part of the attack includes the rushing champ who is going to Super Bowl."

It is, however, an answer that others have been giving for him.

Months later, after MTV host Bill Bellamy taped Super Bowl video introductions with the players, he told *The New York Times*: "Emmitt Smith was very confident. He shook my hand and looked me directly in the eyes. You can tell they are a young, hip team because most everyone in there seemed to know a lot about MTV. But Smith, he had the personality. He had the confidence. It seems to make him a natural leader."

And a natural achiever.

Smith has been the NFL rushing leader for two years now. (He's

ROAD WARRIOR

the first to lead in back-to-back seasons since Eric Dickerson in 1983 and 1984.) In 1991, he carried the football 1,563 yards. In 1992, he gained 1,713 yards. And when the Dallas Cowboys beat San Francisco for the NFC title, he became the first rushing leader in NFL history who would play in the Super Bowl. Before the season started, Smith had set a goal of 2,000 yards for 1992. "If I don't get 2,000 and still win the Super Bowl," he said, "it'll be a successful season." Not to worry. With the 228 yards he gained in playoff games and the 108 (in 22 carries) in the Super Bowl, Smith hit 2049 yards for the year.

As the numbers show, Smith runs long. But as observers from all over have seen, he also runs anywhere he wants—inside or out. Gary Myers of New York's *Daily News* notes, "He always gets through the first tackle." Owner Jerry Jones has described Smith as "a young man with elf eyes," who spots and aims straight for the paydirt.

"He darts, feints, shifts back and forth like a typewriter carriage," wrote the *Philadelphia Inquirer*. "He stops in the hole—comes to a complete stop—looks unhurriedly for a seam and skates across the field like a hot dog wrapper."

The comparisons to football greats—especially Cowboy greats—are irresistible. Over their first 32 games, Smith and Tony Dorsett had almost identical yardage. (Smith was six yards ahead with an even 2,500.) Over his career, Dorsett averaged 17.6 carries and 76.7 yards per game. At the beginning of the 1992 season, Smith was averaging 18.9 carries and 78.1 yards per game.

Smith showed his abilities as soon as he became a Cowboy. He missed training camp in 1990, his

"Awesome."
–Fred
Stokes

first year, over contract differences. But after only a week with the team, he started against the New York Giants. He scored his first touchdown the next week and rushed 17 times for 63 yards against Washington, the best performance by a Cowboy back of the season. "Awesome—there's just one word to describe him," said Washington defensive end Fred Stokes.

"Emmitt Smith is what he's supposed to be," explained Cowboys running backs coach Joe Brodsky. "He got paid $1 million to make people miss, and that's what he did."

Emmitt Smith has been making people miss for quite some time. Following in the footsteps of his father, who played semi-pro ball, Smith was playing tackle games with his cousins at age five and was participating at age seven in a league sponsored by the Salvation Army in his hometown of Pensacola, Florida.

At Escambia High, he racked up 8,804 yards over four years for 106 touchdowns and a 7.8-yard average per carry. In 45 games (all but four of the games he played), Smith carried the ball more than 100 yards. Even as a 5-foot 8-inch, 175-pound

freshman, he rushed for 205 yards against Gulf Breeze High and 210 yards against Niceville High. Smith wound up his prep career as Player of the Year in both *USA Today* and *Parade magazine*.

Smith's career at the University of Florida was just as spectacular—though it lasted only three years. By the seventh game of his freshman year, he had rushed for 1,000 yards. No other collegiate player had achieved that mark so quickly. And Smith joined Herschel Walker as the only freshmen ever to finish in the top 10 in Heisman Trophy balloting. An All American

and a three time All Southeastern Conference pick, Smith established 58 school records, including 3,928 yards rushing.

At the end of his junior year, however, Smith decided to forego the final year of college eligibility for the pros. The Dallas Cowboys, looking to fill the void left by trading Herschel Walker, made him their number-one draft choice in April 1990.

Smith, said Jimmy Johnson, was "top notch. I think he'll make a big impact this year."

What kind of impact did he have? Just take a look:

• 1990, NFL Offensive Rookie of the Year.
• 1991, the first Cowboy to lead the league in rushing.
• 1992, once again, the NFL rushing leader.
• 108 yards and a touchdown in the Super Bowl.
• Youngest player in league history to rush for over 1,500 yards in a season.
• Three-time Pro Bowl selection. First Cowboy to go to back-to-back Pro Bowls since Herschel Walker in 1987-88.
• First player in Cowboy history to post consecutive seasons of 10 or more rushing touchdowns.
• In the 1990 playoffs in Chicago, he rushed for 105 yards. Since 1932, the Bears had never allowed a running back to gain more than 100 yards in a playoff game.

Smith, nonetheless, describes himself as "laid back." And devoted to his family. His mother and sister run Emmitt, Inc., his merchandising company in Pensacola. He's had orders for T-shirts and posters (one set touts "Double-Trouble," Emmitt and wide receiver Michael Irvin) from as far away as Germany and Japan. And just before the Super Bowl, Smith made a quick trip home to autograph souvenirs he sells.

Laid back? Perhaps. After the Cowboys beat defending Super Bowl champs Washington and New York to open the 1992 season, what was his response? "It doesn't mean nothing. It just means we're 2-0."

> *"He has a God-given ability to make people miss."*
> —Troy Aikman

After he tied Tony Dorsett's record of 1,000 yards or more in consecutive seasons and set a team record of 13 touchdowns, what was his response? "What about it? It don't mean nothin'. A lot of things mean more than setting records. Winning is one of them. I'd rather be in the Super Bowl than breaking records."

But Emmitt Smith can do both.

In the playoffs against San Francisco, he got off to a slow start, but wound up with 24 carries and 114 yards. Add pass receptions (he's one of the best receivers at his position), and Smith gained 173, more than any other player in the game. He was Super Bowl Bound.

"It's not where you start, it's where you finish," said Smith, explaining that day. "We finished up strong, strong enough to win the game. Now we've got to put this behind us and go for the big bowl."

Which the Cowboys and Emmitt Smith did.

> *"He always gets through the first tackle."*
> —Gary Meyers

THE SUPER BOWL ROSTER

No.	Player Pos.	Ht.	Wt.	Birthdate	Exp.	College
34	Agee, Tommie FB	6-0	227	2/22/64	5	Auburn
8	Aikman, Troy QB	6-4	222	11/21/66	4	UCLA
7	Beuerlein, Steve QB	6-2	213	3/7/65	5	Notre Dame
24	Brown, Larry CB	5-11	185	11/30/69	2	Texas Christian
75	Casillas, Tony DT	6-3	273	10/26/69	7	Oklahoma
68	Cornish, Frank C-G	6-4	285	9/24/67	3	UCLA
58	Edwards, Dixon LB	6-1	224	3/25/68	2	Michigan State
2	Elliot, Lin K	6-0	182	11/11/68	R	Texas Tech
27	Everett, Thomas S	5-9	183	11/21/64	6	Baylor
39	Gainer, Derrick RB	5-11	240	8/15/66	2	Florida A&M
29	Gant, Kenneth DB	5-11	191	4/18/67	3	Albany State
63	Gesek, John G	6-5	282	2/18/63	6	CSU-Sacr.
66	Gogan, Kevin G-T	6-7	319	11/2/64	6	Washington
94	Haley, Charles DE	6-5	245	1/6/64	7	James Madison
80	Harper, Alvin WR	6-3	207	7/6/67	2	Tennessee
70	Hellestrae, Dale G-C	6-5	283	7/11/62	6	SMU
95	Hennings, Chad DE	6-6	267	10/20/65	R	Air Force
47	Holmes, Clayton CB	5-10	181	8/23/69	R	Carson Newman
30	Holt, Issiac CB	6-2	198	10/4/62	8	Alcorn State
20	Horton, Ray S	5-11	188	4/12/60	10	Washington
88	Irvin, Michael WR	6-2	199	3/5/66	5	Miami
77	Jeffcoat, Jim DE	6-5	276	4/1/61	10	Arizona State
48	Johnston, Daryl FB	6-2	238	2/10/66	4	Syracuse
97	Jones, Jimmie DL	6-4	276	1/9/66	3	Miami
55	Jones, Robert LB	6-2	238	9/27/69	R	East Carolina
78	Lett, Leon DL	6-6	292	10/12/68	2	Emporia State
83	Martin, Kelvin WR-KR	5-9	165	5/14/65	6	Boston College
67	Maryland, Russell DT	6-1	275	3/22/69	2	Miami
98	Myles, Godfrey LB	6-1	242	9/22/68	2	Florida
61	Newton, Nate G	6-3	303	12/20/61	7	Florida A&M
51	Norton, Ken LB	6-2	241	9/29/66	5	UCLA
84	Novacek, Jay TE	6-4	231	10/24/62	8	Wyoming
52	Pruitt, Mickey LB	6-1	218	1/10/65	5	Colorado
4	Saxon, Mike P	6-3	200	7/10/62	8	San Diego State
22	Smith, Emmitt RB	5-9	209	5/15/69	3	Florida
82	Smith, Jimmy WR	6-1	205	2/9/69	R	Jackson State
26	Smith, Kevin CB	5-11	177	4/7/70	R	Texas A&M
57	Smith, Vinson LB	6-2	237	7/3/65	4	East Carolina
53	Stepnoski, Mark C	6-2	269	1/20/67	4	Pittsburgh
89	Tennell, Derek TE	6-5	270	2/12/64	5	UCLA
92	Tolbert, Tony DE	6-6	265	12/29/67	4	Texas-El Paso
71	Tuinei, Mark T	6-5	298	3/31/60	10	Hawaii
76	Veingrad, Alan G-T	6-5	280	7/24/63	6	East Texas State
37	Washington, James S	6-1	203	1/10/65	5	UCLA
79	Williams, Erik T	6-6	321	9/7/68	2	Central State Ohio
23	Williams, Robert DB	5-10	186	10/2/62	6	Baylor
28	Woodson, Darren S	6-1	215	4/25/69	R	Arizona State

OH, BOYS!

SUPER HEROES

Celebration

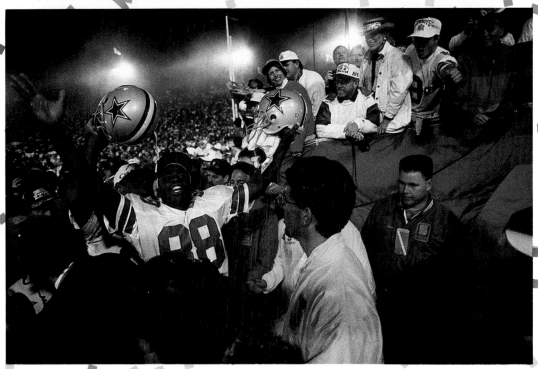

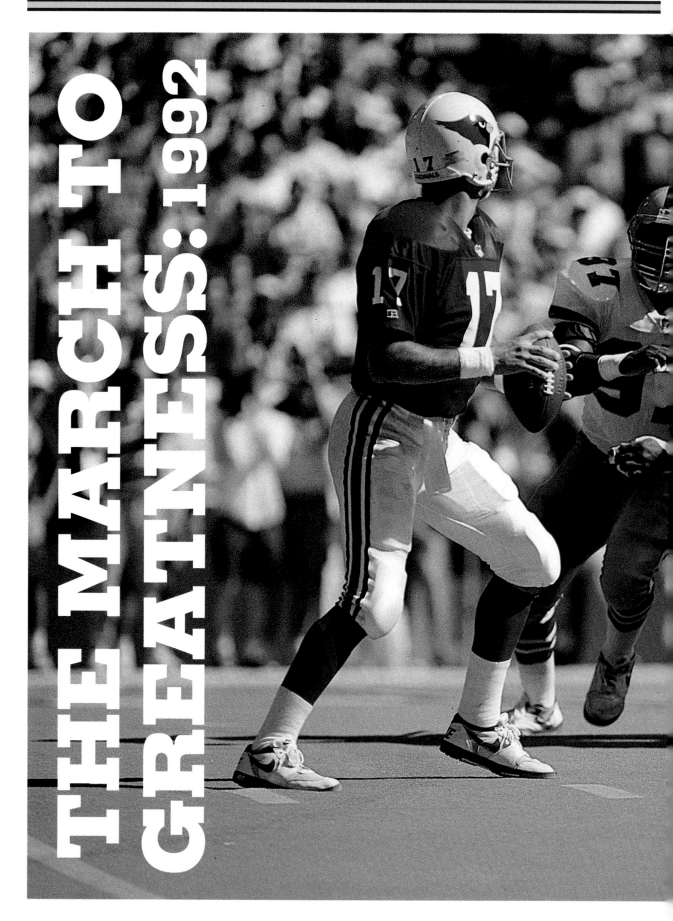

THE MARCH TO GREATNESS: 1992

The Cowboys and their fans had a taste of playoffs in 1991— and found it a heady, intoxicating experience. Downright addictive, if the truth be told. Obsessive. Passionate. Unstoppable. And by 1992, they were ready for the good times again. They had known success. And they remembered how much they had missed it.

Everyone seemed to understand by now, however, that a winning team like the Cowboys included more—a lot more—than heart-stopping, tackle-dodging, pass-grabbing superstars. There can be only one Troy Aikman. One Michael Irvin. One Emmitt Smith. Besides, head coach Jimmy Johnson had a plan. To build the team around his running backs. And this was the final year he would be able to draw on 1989's much-ballyhooed Herschel Walker trade.

Johnson stuck to that plan in April, when he drafted only one receiver—and eight players for the line or the defense. Sure, the top pick, Texas A&M cornerback Kevin Smith, was known for big plays in the defensive secondary. The Cowboys took two safeties and another cornerback, too. But the new crop also was stocked with guards, tackles and linebackers. Jimmy Johnson said about the 1992 draft, "The quality of this draft is better than what we've seen since I've been with the Cowboys."

So, it should be no surprise, then, that 1992 was the year that the Cowboys' defense ranked number one in the NFL. Probably because they worked so well as a unit, no defensive player was named to the Pro Bowl team—an oversight that angered many. But the Pro Bowl disappointment just proved that young veteran linebacker Ken Norton, Jr., was right when he said, "Our defense is getting famous for not being famous."

As usual, the Cowboys received their share of criticism from pre-season pundits who said their players were too young to achieve much. Instead, Washington and Philadelphia were the favorites to win the NFC title.

"Our defense is getting famous for not being famous."

–Ken Norton Jr.

Some people were even saying the Cowboys would slip back to 8 and 8. *Sport* magazine called the team defense "suspect." And it almost appeared the critics might be right when the Cowboys lost veteran middle linebacker Jack Del Rio to the Minnesota Vikings because they hadn't protected him in the Plan B draft. A bitter Del Rio, something of a fixture in Dallas, complained, "All the emphasis is on the young guys and the future." Johnson pointedly responded: "We will be better than ever next season at linebacker." And with the emergence of veteran Ken Norton, Jr., as the team's leading tackler, Johnson was proven correct.

Of course, Johnson was right about other things. Lots of them. Before the season he irritated many by saying, "Not only do I knew we're going to win, but our players know it, and everyone in the NFL knows it. I'm sure there are a few skeptics out there in the league, but it's not the majority. A big part of winning is when you and everyone else knows it's going to happen."

The skeptics, it should be noted for the record, were noticeably quiet by the end of the season.

In an interview with the *Orange County Register* in California just before the Super Bowl, even Tom Landry admitted he wasn't surprised at the Cowboys' resurgence. He credited the draft.

"They were very fortunate," he said. "Our last year we were 3-13, so they ended up getting the first draft choice and taking Troy Aikman. I would have taken

Aikman, too. Then they got all those picks when they traded Herschel Walker to Minnesota. I guess they can thank [former Vikings General Manager] Mike Lynn for that trade. That's the thing. You can't turn around a team that fast without a lot of players and some luck. It works very well for them, and that's fine. The breaks went their way."

The turnaround had taken more than breaks, however. It had taken smarts. And it would take more smarts as the season went on.

It would take smarts from coaches. Two weeks before the season started, Johnson traded two draft picks for yet another defenseman—Charles Haley, a pass-rush specialist and former Pro Bowler from San Francisco who *Sports Illustrated* said "could come around the corner at 90 mph." Haley had 63 career sacks to his credit. "I think everybody knows we've been looking for a pass rusher the last couple of years," said Johnson. "I think we have improved significantly with

our pass rush, but Charles Haley improves it that much more." Combined with the resident rushers—popular 10-year Cowboy Jim Jeffcoat and revitalized Tony Casillas and solid Tony Tolbert—the 'Boys were about to become a major source of quarterback headaches around the league. Not that opposing runners would have a cakewalk against the rest of the defensive line, which included a crop of bright new stars, including Russell Maryland (out of the University of Miami), Leon Lett, Jimmie Jones (whom Johnson had recruited at Miami), and Chad Hennings (a pilot fresh from the Gulf War).

And it would take smarts from the players. Offensive tackle Nate Newton, long the butt of fat jokes, reported for training camp 60 pounds lighter than he had finished the previous season. Some players and coaches didn't even recognize him. Neither did his opponents. At 305 pounds, Newton proved to be a more agile, more effective player than ever. As light-

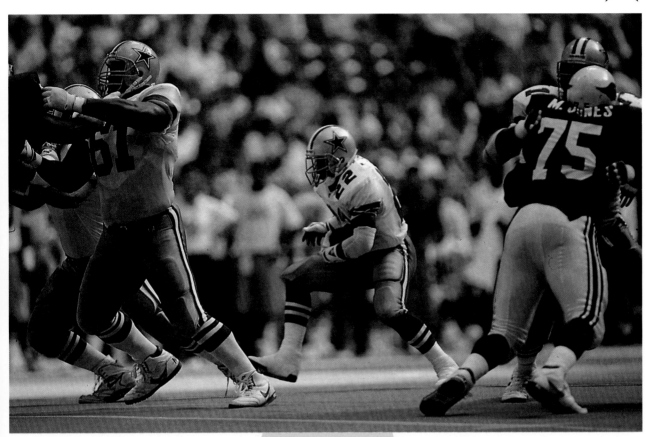

hearted as he was heavy-footed, the ebullient Newton was the beef on a rejuvenated offensive line, which included solid vets Mark Tuinei, Kevin Gogan and John Gesek, plus young star Erik Williams, named to *Sports Illustrated's* All Pro team by resident football guru Paul Zimmerman.

The team was ready to play.

And what a marvelous season it would be.

The Cowboys would lead off by beating the defending Super Bowl champs. Then the Super Bowl champs from the year before. During the course of the regular season and playoffs, in fact, the Cowboys would beat every team that had won a Super Bowl since 1982.

Here's how it unfolded:

On an early September Monday evening in Dallas, a Rangers home baseball game forced local fans to choose between sports. But those like country music star Charlie Pride who picked football saw a classic, as Dallas defeated arch-

rival Washington, the defending Super Bowl champions. Issiac Holt, a cornerback who came to Dallas from Minnesota in the Herschel Walker bonanza, was the first to put the Cowboys on the 1992 scoreboard, blocking a Washington punt out of the end zone for a safety. Emmitt Smith rushed for 139 yards and a touchdown on 27 carries. Final score: 23-10. The Redskins, defending Super Bowl champions, had been a two-point favorite. The Cowboys, before a national audience, had served notice.

The following Sunday, on the road, the Cowboys ran up a 34-point lead in three quarters against another favorite, the legendary New York Giants, then almost lost it before time ran out. This time, Ken Norton, Jr., blocked a punt and safety Robert Williams ran it in for a touchdown. But the defense faded as the Giants ran four successful scoring drives in the fourth quarter. Final score: 34-28. It was a close call. But "all's well that ends well." The Cowboys

had beaten another Super Bowl champ.

And counting wins at the end of the 1991 season, Dallas now had a seven-game winning streak. They were a force to be reckoned with.

Dallas hadn't lost to Phoenix since 1989, when they lost to everybody. And this year, with the Cardinals turning in a 4-12 season for last place in the NFC East, was no exception. The Cowboys took a game at home 31-20 and a game on the road 16-10.

In the first game, at Dallas in September, Michael Irvin caught his first touchdown pass when the game was only 61 seconds old. Two more followed. In all, Irvin caught eight passes—one for an 87-yard score—and set a personal record of 210 yards. Emmitt Smith added another touchdown and rushed for 112 yards, becoming the first Cowboy rusher to break 100 in five straight home games.

In Tempe in November, Phoenix went up 7-0 in the first quarter but didn't get much farther, as the

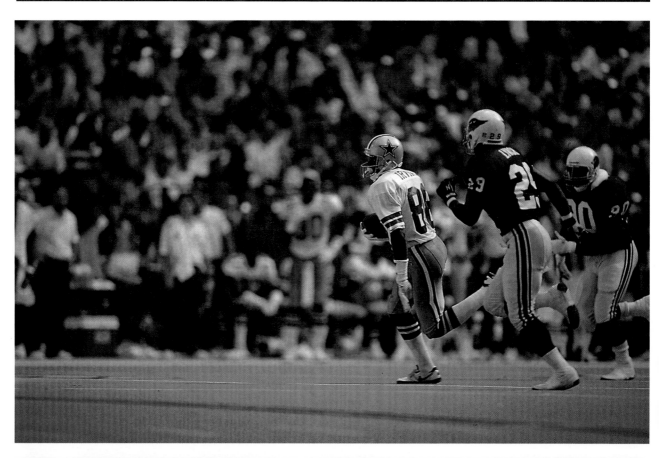

Cowboy defense gave up only 149 yards and nine first downs. Rookie kicker Lin Elliott tied a team record with his ninth straight field goal. And Troy Aikman threw a season-high 25 completions, including touchdown passes to rock-steady Jay Novacek and the spectacular Alvin Harper.

The Cowboys had long had trouble with Philadelphia. In the three years since the changing of the guard in Dallas, the teams had met six times—and Dallas had won only once. But that was their most recent meeting, the second game of 1991. And the Eagles were out for revenge. "A bigger sporting event has never taken place," declared one over-heated disk jockey in the City of Brotherly Love. For one thing, Herschel Walker, the former Cowboy, was now an Eagle.

Philadelphia had its way at home on October 5, handing Dallas its first loss of the season. Michael Irvin went 105 yards and Emmitt Smith 67, but the Cowboys committed four turnovers, three of which ended up as Eagle touchdowns. When the game was over, Herschel Walker was predicting an unbeaten Philadelphia season. (On the road against Kansas City and Washington, their lost the next two games.)

On November 1 in Dallas, it was the Cowboys' turn for revenge. Emmitt Smith carried the ball 30 times for 163 yards, including a 51-yarder and a total of 115 in the second half. It was the first time any running back had gone over 100 yards against Philadelphia in 53 games. "I always say, as Emmitt goes, so go the Cowboys," declared Eagles safety Wes Hopkins. The final score: 20-10.

Dallas' victory over Philadelphia produced another phenomenon: the Cowboy defense, which held the Eagles to only 189 yards, was now ranked number one in the NFL. The previous leader? Philadelphia.

By season's end, the Dallas D was giving up an average of only 245.8 yards per game and only 77.8 yards rushing. The D surrendered only 241 first downs and a third-down conversion success rate of 27.2 percent. All were league bests.

"Last year," Emmitt Smith

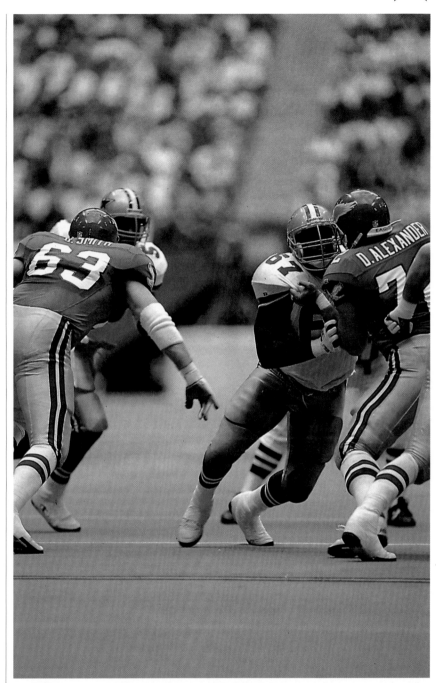

"(The defense is) suspect."
–Sport *Magazine*

"I think we have a Super Bowl caliber team."
–*Jimmy Johnson*

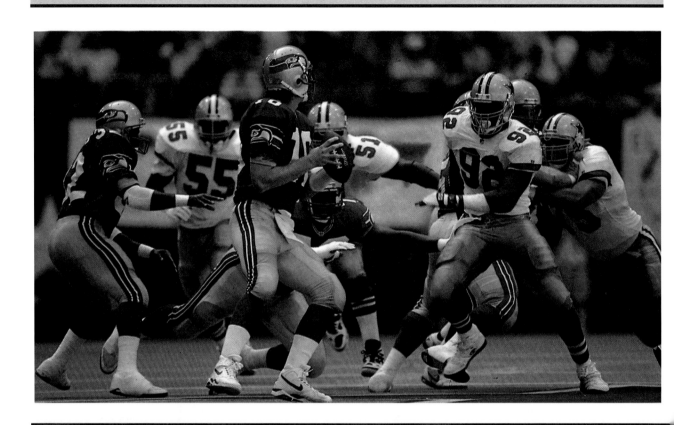

After this blowout, Seattle coach Tom Flores

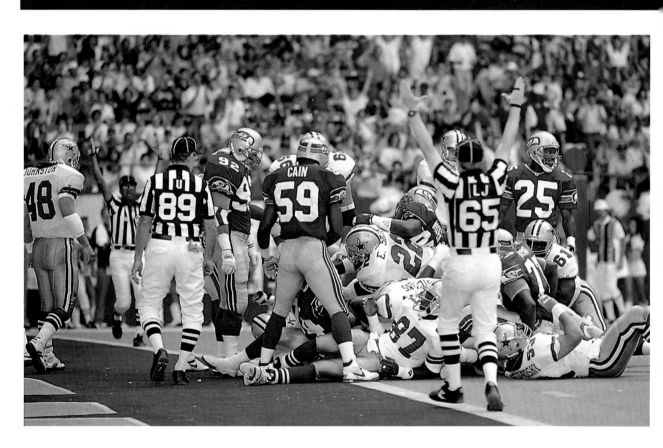

said, "We just want to get out of town."

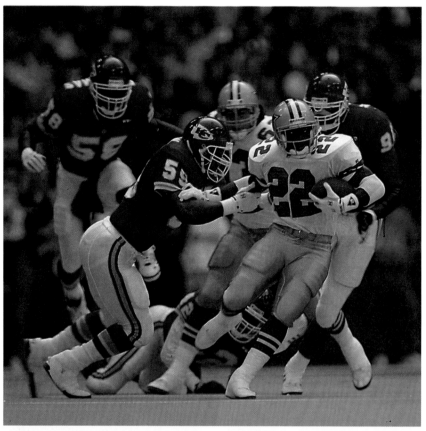

observed, "it seemed like it could be third-and-21 and the other team would get 22 yards. It's not happening this year. Our defense is playing great. That's a big reason for our turnaround."

Many attributed the defense's own turnaround to the arrival of Charles Haley. Said New Orleans linebacker Pat Swilling, a Pro Bowl pass rusher, "Without a doubt, Haley is what made their defense happen. He gives them the pressure they didn't have."

In other defensive developments, safety Kenneth Gant borrowed a few moves from cornerback Kevin Smith and popularized a celebration dance he called "The Shark."

And by the end of the season, the Cowboys' resident defensive genius coach, Dave Wannstedt, had been named head coach of the Chicago Bears.

The Cowboys' racked up big victories against non-NFC East opponents:

27-0 over Seattle (the defense surrendered a startlingly low 62 yards in the Cowboys first regular-season shutout in 14 years).

17-10 over Kansas City (the win landed them atop the NFC East for the first time since 1986).

28-13 over Oakland (Emmitt Smith's 152 yards and three touchdowns earned him NFC Offensive Player of the Week honors before a crowd of 91,895 in Los Angeles, the largest to attend a Cowboys game to date).

37-3 over Detroit (the victory dropped the defending NFC Central champions to 2-7 and avenged two Cowboy losses to the Lions in 1991).

31-27 over Denver (Emmitt Smith scored his 16th touchdown of the season, tying a team record set in 1966 by Dan Reeves—now the Bronco coach).

Then the Cowboys sputtered against the Los Angeles Rams. Emmitt Smith broke the touchdown record he had tied in Denver with his 13th score, and he became the first Cowboy to rush for more than 1,000 yards in back-to-back seasons since Tony Dorsett (1984-85). But while Dallas led into the fourth quarter, the Rams kicked

Michael Irvin flying downfield against the L.A. Raiders. In the 28-13 Cowboy victory, Emmitt Smith contributed 152 rushing yards and three touchdowns. The ground and air attack was devastating.

two field goals to take the game, 27-23.

Nonetheless, there was a lot of jubilation among the Cowboys at mid-season. After the Kansas City victory, played in Dallas, coach Jimmy Johnson declared, "I think we have a Super Bowl-caliber team."

After defeating the Raiders in California, owner Jerry Jones was thinking Super Bowl, too. "Maybe we've gotten used to playing in Los Angeles," he said. "We'll see."

On Thanksgiving Day, the Cowboys stuffed the Giants, the first time they had beaten New York twice in a season since 1987. With a 68-yard touchdown run, Emmitt Smith also became the first Cowboy since Tony Dorsett (1980) to rush for 100 yards against New York. Lin Elliott kicked three field goals for a team-record 12 straight. Final score: 30-3.

But the Cowboys' meeting with Washington was a different story. Leading in the fourth quarter, they first gave up an interception that allowed a Redskin field goal. Minutes later, Aikman lost the ball while attempting to pass from his own end zone. Emmitt Smith

grabbed the ball but his toss to Alfredo Roberts misfired. Recovered by Washington in the end zone, the ball was ruled a fumble—and a touchdown. Final score: 20-13.

"We felt like we had the ball game and let it get away from us," Aikman said. "I should have taken better care of the ball."

Despite Aikman's post-game conservatism, this was the same sort of trademark Cowboy risk taking that won other games—including the playoff against the 49ers. And it illustrated the gambling Cowboys' go-for-it, never-play-it-safe philosophy. It showed they are unpredictable—like their coach. And never boring.

Against Atlanta, Troy Aikman hit a career-high 13 straight passes (18 of 21 total) to win 41-17 and secure the NFC East. Emmitt Smith carried 24 times for 174 yards, topping 1,500 for the second consecutive year and 4,000 yards for his career. He scored twice, raising his team TD record to 18. Jay Novacek, who would wind up the season leading the NFL tight ends in receiving yards (630) and receptions (68), caught five passes to set a team record for tight ends. Guard Tony Casillas, who once played for Atlanta but had been the recipient of scorn from Coach Jerry Glanville, who traded him to Dallas, declared after the game, "I want to thank Jerry for putting me in his doghouse and the whole Atlanta organization for giving me this opportunity."

And, finally, in Chicago, in a game that didn't matter any more, the Cowboys played like it mattered, scoring 24 points in the third quarter and winning 27-14. The 13th regular-season victory was a team record. Emmitt Smith was named NFC Player of the Week with 131 yards and took the NFL rushing title with 1,713 yards for the season. And defensive tackle Russell Maryland grabbed a botched pitchout and raced 26 yards for his first touchdown. The 277-pounder spiked the ball and did a belly flop in the end zone. "Kenny Gant has the shark," he said after the game. "I guess that was the killer whale."

PHILLY FALLS:
THE DIVISIO

Yes, the Dallas Cowboys had the second-best record in the National Football League going into the playoffs. But their recent post-season experience as a team was practically nil, and most of that was bad-memory stuff.

Let the questions begin.

Start with 1991. The 'Boys squeaked by an old and declining Chicago Bear team that itself had squeaked into the post-season tourney. Score: 17-13. Then it was on to Detroit. Uh, oh.

In the Pontiac Superdome true football ugliness occurred. The final score was 38-6. (And looking back, the Lions didn't exactly turn out to be a rising NFL superpower. Their '92 record was 5-11.) Don't scars take time to heal? And isn't playoff experience crucial to future success?

Baloney, Troy Aikman would say—Ache-man after the Lions got through with him last year—whose playoff experience amounted to a half in that Michigan massacre. And he did say it in his gentlemanly way: "I personally feel playoff experience is overrated." (A skeptic might have observed: What else would he say?)

There were other things to worry about. The Eagles, rough and ready, were on a roll after stumbling and squabbling in mid-season. And these same mayhem-minded souls had applied to the Cowboys their worst beating of the '92 season in game four. In the 31-7 blowout, the trash-talking Philly DBs mugged every wide receiver they saw, and the top-ranked defense set up three scores with two interceptions and a fumble recovery. Adding to the indignity, much-maligned ex-Cowboy Herschel Walker ran for 86 yards with two touchdowns.

"Philadelphia is the most talent-ed team in the league," Jimmy Johnson said afterward.

Now, in the playoffs, Dallas would be hosting the Eagles, who weren't acting the polite guests. Truculent Andre Waters, a noted cheap-shot artist, had taken offense when Emmitt Smith had called him...a cheap-shot artist. If the shoe fits....

"Two of us are going to walk on the field," Waters said about Smith, "but only one of us is going to walk off. They're going to have to carry him off."

Nice. Or, as it turned out, nice and dumb.

There were other potential Cowboy problems. The once sputtering Philadelphia offense (things got so bad All Pro Randall Cunningham even lost his starting job for a game) had come vibrantly alive. Against a superb New Orleans defense in the wild card game the week before, the Eagles had rolled up 36 points. Philly's rushing offense was second in the NFC, a powerful complement to Cunningham's sweet throwing. The Dallas No-Name Defense was about to be tested.

Did we mention the Eagles flew into Dallas with a five-game winning streak?

But Jimmy Johnson was not worrying. He told his team during the week before the game that if they prepared properly, the game was "a done deal." His confidence

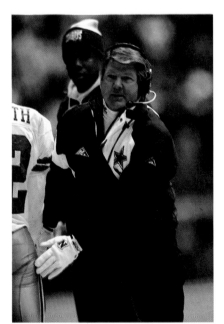 

"Playoff experience is overrated."
– Troy Aikman

Who says Troy can't run?

Daryl Johnston. Full bore, all the time. The Bill Bates of the offense.

was such that he even inquired during the week about "muddying" up a practice feel to prepare for San Francisco the following week. This sort of foresight is coaching heresy, but as with so many things Johnson often ignores the norm and isn't afraid to admit it. "I broke one of my own rules by doing that, by looking ahead," he would say later.

Not that Philadelphia was doing a shrinking-violet turn. Tight end Keith Byars predicted the Eagles would beat the Cowboys, and what's more the Redskins would defeat the 49ers to give the Eagles the home field advantage in the NFC championship game. Whoops.

On Sunday, January 10, thanks, at least in part, to the brain-locked braggadocio of various Philly wide-mouths, Texas Stadium rocked like Buddy Holly in his prime. The rocking actually had begun the night before, over at injured safety Bill Bates' ranch north of Dallas. It was wet and cool, not a pretty night, but 10,000 wild folks didn't seem to notice. The police did…they had to, since the traffic was backed up six miles just trying

Irvin & Harper. Playmaking brothers.

to reach Bates' spread. Bates told the throng he threw the rally as a way of "thanking you and getting you primed for the game on Sunday."

"What are we going to do to the Eagles on Sunday?" Bates hollered. "We're going to roast them, right?" The crowd cheered and hollered right back. Primed? No problem.

Politicians, being politicians, got involved in the excitement. A $1,000 wager between the two cities' mayors was spiced up by Steve Bartlett's specific prediction: 28-13. Not bad, Mr. Mayor. (Any chance we'll hear about that come next election? Go ahead...you earned it.)

The day started like a page from Eagle coach Rich Kotite's personal diary. March down the field, dominate, get on the board. Roger Ruzek's 32-yard field goal put Philly ahead. But from that point on, Kotite's fantasy got a rude wake-up call. The 'Boys kicked into gear when Kelvin Martin scooted 39 yards with the kickoff. Dallas drove an efficient 46 yards for a touchdown, the six coming on a pass to tight end Derek Tennell

Efficient Offense

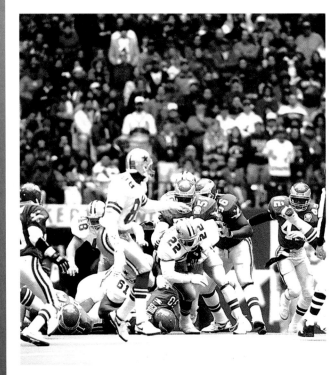

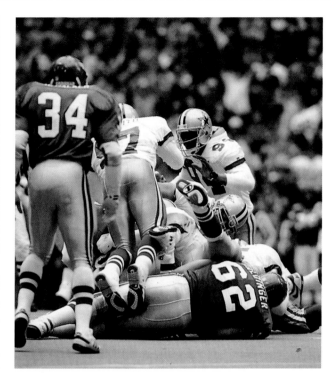

Dominant Defense

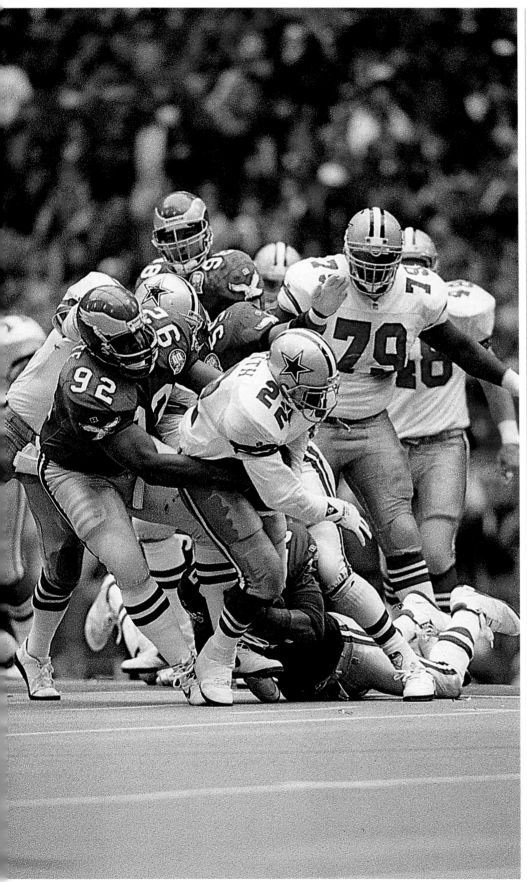

(signed as a free agent ten days before to replace the injured Alfredo Roberts.)

From that point on the Cowboys scored early and often. The quiet cowboy, tight end Jay Novacek, grabbed a six-yarder from Aikman to make it 14-3 as the half wound down. Alvin Harper, beginning a playoff run to stardom, had snagged a 41-yard bomb to set up Novacek's score. Then Philadelphia's lethal weapon, Vai Sikahema, exploded on contact; his fumble produced a 20-yard Lin Elliott field goal. In the last 47 seconds of the half, the Cowboys had thrown 10 points of gasoline on a simmering fire.

"There's no question about it," Kotite said, "it was a big plus for them."

The pluses multiplied in the second half. Emmitt Smith, as he had so often during 1992, accelerated his pace in the second half. To warp speed. Andre Waters was scalded for a 23-yard TD as part of Smith's 69-yard third-quarter total.

"What can I say?" Waters would offer later. "Today he showed he was a great running back."

Scoring contributions were made by reserve running back Derrick Gainer with a one-yard burst and by Lin Elliott with another field goal.

Troy Aikman, who completed 15 of 25 passes, including 10 of his last 13 for two touchdowns, was named the NFL's Offensive Player of the Week.

"I don't think they get all the credit they deserve," Eagle quarterback Randall Cunningham said after the game. Randall's perspective was up close and personal. The finest running QB in the game had been sacked five times and harassed incessantly. "We came after them," said veteran Jim Jeffcoat. "We made plays." The youth of America's Team was a bit cockier. "We could have done better," said defensive tackle Russell Maryland. "We could have shut them out."

The Doomsday Defense, long dormant, was risen. "Every time I saw somebody open for a second, the Cowboys were back in my face," said Cunningham.

Jimmy Johnson called it a "super, super victory." And then reminded his team that "you're one game from the Super Bowl."

Cunningham seemed a believer. "They are a great team," he said, "and today they whipped our butts. They're a young team, and they'll be around for a while, and others better get used to them."

"It's a big win for us," Coach Johnson said. "We've got bigger wins coming."

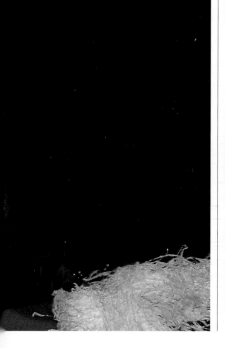

RETURN TO THE MOUNTAINTOP:

The NFC Champions

ometimes, life can be perfect. In fact, so perfect that it makes you nervous.

Take, for example, the 1992-93 National Football Conference Championship Game, January 17, 1993, in Candlestick Park, San Francisco, California.

A game whose symmetry was, for Cowboys fans, downright eerie.

Over 10 long years before, these same two teams—moving rapidly in opposite directions—had met in the same stadium to play for the NFC Championship. It was a game that would make NFL history. The Drive. The Catch. Dwight Clark. The making of a legend—Joe Montana, the best in the game. Maybe, the best ever.

It was a spectacular football battle. The beginning of a decade-long Dallas Cowboy nightmare. And the start of a San Francisco 49er dynasty that would last 10 years and more.

The losing Cowboys would begin a free-fall into the NFL's version of Death Valley, a fall that would not bottom out until the shock and embarrassment of 1989. 1-15. The Dallas Cowboys? America's Team? Not possible.

Now fast forward to 1993. The 49ers, still dominant after all these years, defending the NFC Championship against the brash young Cowboys. It had been 10 years since the Cowboys had been anywhere within hollering distance

of this game...but most experts agreed they just weren't ready. Success for Jones and Johnson, Aikman, Smith & Company had come too quickly. Timing is everything in life, and this timing was wrong.

Which goes to show just how wrong the experts can be.

And consider the following oddity: That infamous 1981 NFC Championship? Out of five post-season games, it was the only time the 49ers had ever beaten the Cowboys.

January 1993 was the wettest month in northern California history. Candlestick Park, below sea level, was soaked and sodden, prompting local wits to label it the "Field of Streams." The condition of the playing surface became national news, a "Sod Saga." Ace groundskeeper George Toma—a.k.a. The Sod God—was brought in to make the field playable. Toma took one look at "Candleslop" and called it "the worst field I've ever seen."

"Everybody is making a big deal out of the field, but I've run in water and mud before," Emmitt Smith responded. "I'm prepared for any style."

But most thought the drenched field favored the 49ers, who 1) were familiar with their home turf and 2) had, in effect, three full-time runners to rely on: Ricky Watters (over 1,000 rushing yards), fullback Tom Rathman and Steve Young, the finest rushing quarterback since...Roger Staubach. Against the Washington Redskins, in the NFC divisional playoff the week before, the elusive Young had rolled up 278 yards of offense on the slippery sod. "I like this kind of

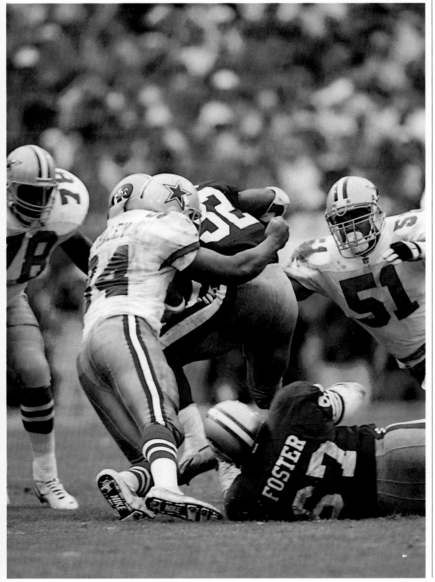

"I've run in mud and water before."

—Emmitt Smith

son; arguably he is the greatest pass-catcher in NFL history. The offense Young and Rice led was the league's best. Oh, their record? 15-2, the league's best.

This is called an embarrassment of riches.

But the 49ers had liabilities, too. Their defense was ranked No. 4 against the rush, but No. 26 against the pass, for an over-all ranking of 15th in the NFL. The much-maligned 49er secondary took its lumps in '92, allowing 210.6 passing yards per game and giving up 20 touchdowns via the air. The 49er secondary coach, Eric Wright, who had started in the 49ers' last Super Bowl victory in 1989 (a 55-10 blowout of the Denver Broncos), saw his charges improve as the season went on, allowing only one passing touchdown in their last five games. "They are good," Wright said. "They are going to get better."

How good was the question. The Cowboy triumvirate of receivers featured two big, rangy weapons in Pro Bowler Michael Irvin (17.9 yards per catch) and Alvin Harper (16.1 average), plus a small speed merchant, Kelvin Martin (11.2 average). (The 'shape' of this group is remarkably similar to that of Buffalo's trio of Andre Reed and James Lofton (big) and Don Beebe (fast). With Troy Aikman at the helm, the Cowboy passing game was likely to severely test San Francisco.

There were other storm clouds forming in Candlestick. The biggest thunderhead was Charles Haley, the seething Cowboy with a score to settle. A six-year 49er veteran, Haley was dealt by the team after a '91 season that saw him make the Pro Bowl. He also wore two Super Bowl rings…and, rumor had it, a perpetual frown—when he wasn't glaring.

When he got to Dallas, Haley's glare reappeared quickly. Owner Jerry Jones picked him up at the airport and said, "Charles, I know you're in Dallas now, but are you leaving your heart in San Francisco?"

Bingo…The Glare. Later came a solitary sentence: "I didn't leave

field," Young said, "It gives me an edge."

The 49ers as a group presented the ultimate challenge. The "Team of the Eighties" had moved seamlessly into the nineties. Coaching legend Bill Walsh was replaced by stoic George Seifert, who quickly won a Super Bowl. When everybody's All-Time quarterback, Joe Montana, went down with a career-threatening back injury, he was replaced by backup Young. The backup was only the NFL's

top-ranked quarterback during the 1992 season. All-Pro, the AP's Player of the Year, 49er MVP. His passing rating was 107.0, the league's best, and he threw for 25 touchdowns. (Meanwhile, Joe Montana was activated for the last game of 1992, ready to produce further miracles should Young stumble. Idle for two years, Montana came in…and promptly threw two touchdown passes.) Wide receiver Jerry Rice set a career record for touchdowns late in the 1992 sea-

anything in San Francisco."

But Charles Haley brought something to Dallas. Besides his enormous talent. Anger. Lots of it.

"To get this whole thing behind me, I need to close the book's chapter. I have a lot of frustration and anger in me that the only way to get it out is to play them."

During the regular season, Haley, often double-teamed, led the Cowboys with 42 quarterback hurries, and added six sacks. Before the NFC championship game, he was quoted in The New York Times as saying, "I don't try and intimidate people but maybe they are by this fact: If you throw a rock at me, I'm coming back at you with a boulder."

Psychological edge: Dallas.

And there were other edges. The bad weather and bad field conditions would mean more than the usual fatigue. The Cowboys defense uses 17 or more men in a regular rotation; it was less likely they would be tired in the second half. Plus, that defense was on a roll. In blowing out Philadelphia 34-10, they had given up to Randall Cunningham and Company a mere 178 total yards and only one out of 11 third-down conversions. Another edge.

Game day was typical San Francisco weather…liquid sunshine, the natives call it; the rest of us call it precipitation. Said Joe Starkey, a sportscaster on KGO radio: "It's rainy, it's ugly, it's awful. It's perfect football weather." Jimmy Johnson played meteorologist, too: "It's not exactly a beautiful day, but hopefully it will be in four hours."

The game began with every Cowboy fan's worst nightmare. A Jerry Rice bomb. On the third play Rice got loose, beating Issiac Holt for a 63-yard touchdown. "I was in the end zone giving high fives," Rice said later, "and noticed that my teammates weren't celebrating." Any joy lasted mere seconds; lying in the scrimmage-line mud was a yellow flag. Holding called on All-Pro guard Guy McIntyre. It was the first 49er mistake, and would not be the last.

"It takes a lot out of a team when you lose a big play like that," said Rice.

The next miscue resulted in the game's first score. San Francisco's Alan Grant grabbed a short Mike Saxon punt on the dead run and was immediately slammed by linebacker Dixon Edwards. Fumble. Daryl Johnston recovered on the San Francisco 22. Taking over on offense, Aikman went for the jugular on the next play, hitting Michael Irvin, who made a spectacular catch, on the one. But big

Michael Carter stopped Emmitt Smith at point blank range, and after two incomplete passes, the 'Boys had to settle for a 20-yard field goal from Lin Elliot. There was 8:20 left in the first quarter.

The inefficiency was an indication of what to expect from the Cowboy offense in the first half. Not much. The 49ers controlled the line of scrimmage, nailing Aikman for four first-half sacks.

Rookie Lin Elliott. Pressure? What pressure?

85

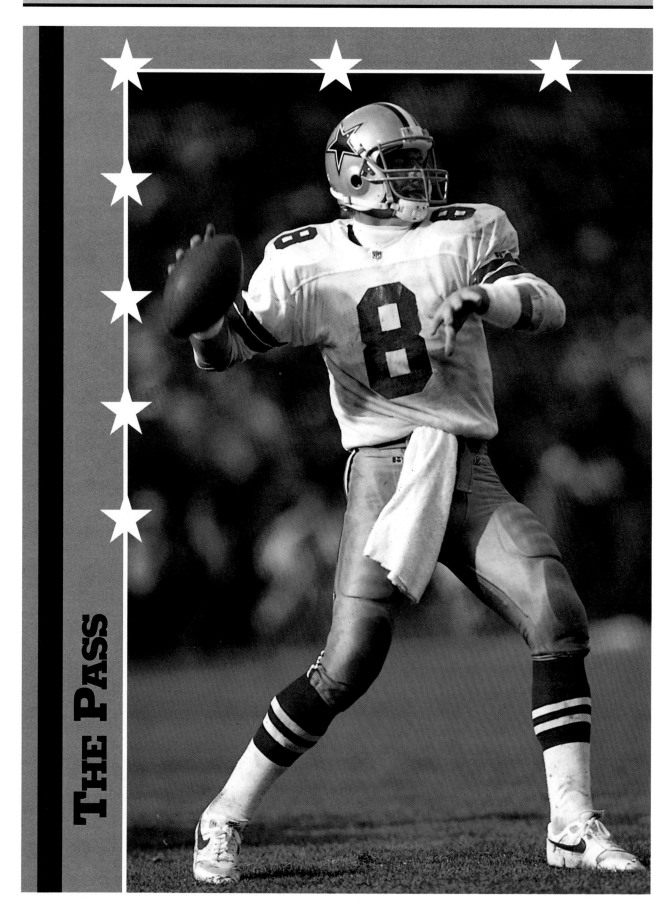

THE PASS

THE CATCH

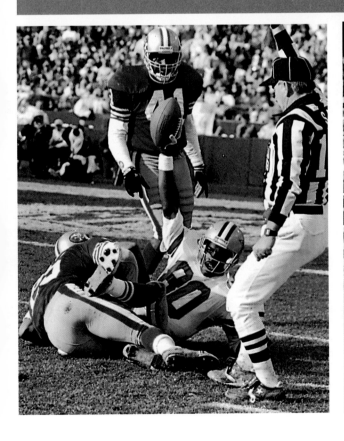

Meanwhile, the San Francisco offense struck back. After the field goal, Mark Logan returned the kickoff 50 yards to the Cowboys 48. Young crisply moved his team. Pass to Rathman for 10 yards. A Watters 16-yard run. Passes to Watters and Rice, and it was third and inches for a goal. Young ran the ball on a keeper and the 49ers led 7-3.

On the sidelines the volatile young Cowboys erupted. Ken Norton, Jr. screamed at teammates James Washington and Thomas Everett...who screamed right back. Coach Dave Campo calmed his troops.

The first quarter ended at 7-3. With the Cowboys doing a solid imitation of the bickering Buffalo Bills, old "Mo Mentum" was in the 49er camp.

Early in the second quarter Mike Cofer, the 49ers' up-and-down field goal kicker, missed from the 47. Then, after Dallas was again thwarted on offense, another break. Mike Saxon boomed his best punt of the day, 49 yards, and San Francisco took over. On first down, Ricky Watters took an inside hand-off and cut back left for fifteen good yards before being popped hard by Larry Brown. Watters coughed up the ball and cornerback Kevin Smith recovered and returned it to the 'Frisco 39-yard line.

Then the Emmitt Smith show started. Left side for four. Then outside, behind Daryl Johnston's block for 15 more. Another four-yarder by Smith. A six-yard Aikman toss to Johnston, and three more to Smith. Now it was third and seven, and one of the game's biggest plays pending. A play fake by Aikman to Smith fooled no one, and the quarterback was forced to throw the ball out of the end zone and settle for a field goal. But, as it turned out, some-one was fooled. San Francisco's Pierce Holt had tackled Emmitt Smith coming out of the backfield.

Smith rushed an official, shouting that he'd been tackled. A moment later came the holding call from a second official. "I told you so," Smith crowed. Another mon-ster mistake from the normally mistake-free Niners. From there it was a walk in the park; a four-yard run by Smith after a textbook-perfect block by Daryl Johnston. 10-7 Cowboys.

But the 49ers came back immediately. Rice, per usual, played the major part with a 26-yard gainer to the Dallas 34. After Rathman hit for 11 yards and Amp Lee for seven, the 49ers were knocking on the door at the 16. Then, with a first down on the 12, tackle Tony Casillas made a huge play, downing Young with the first of his three sacks. Later, Charles Haley blocked a Young pass and the Niners were forced to kick a 28-yard field goal.

The Cowboys made a late stab before the half, Irvin making a diving catch at the 14 and rolling out of bounds to stop the clock. But Aikman was sacked with 20 seconds left by Tim Harris. The loss made Elliott's field goal a 43-yarder, which he missed.

Halftime score: 10-10. The 49ers, most agreed, had had the better of the play. But oh, those turnovers. "I was concerned with the fact that we didn't control the game in the first half," said 49er coach Seifert.

"It never entered my mind," Johnson said, "that we wouldn't win."

The second half would prove to be a classic.

The Cowboys seemed to share Johnson's faith. At halftime Norv Turner changed...nothing. "It wasn't a matter of making adjustments," Aikman said, "it was a matter of execution." And the Niners would be the victims.

Dallas took the opening kickoff and moved 78 yards in eight plays for a touchdown. Alvin Harper's spectacular, leaping catch over Eric Davis was, arguably, the finest individual play of the game. The 38-yard catch put the ball on the seven. Smith ran wide right for four yards, then Daryl Johnston bruised his way three yards for the touchdown. 17-10, Cowboys.

But San Francisco, once again, showed the heart and guts of a champion. Their drive right back at Dallas was the sort of statement that, if not made, means the tide has turned. Instead they rolled against the NFL's best defense, led by a 15-yard run by Watters and a 36-yard pass to who else? Jerry Rice.

But again Tony Casillas came to the rescue. Russell Maryland and Tony Tolbert flushed Young from the pocket, and Casillas promptly claimed his second sack. Instead of a heartening touchdown, the Niners had to settle for a 42-yard goal field by Cofer. 17-13.

Now came the drive of the game. It was time for the offense to stake a Cowboy claim in Pasadena. Led by cool-gun Troy Aikman, who completed seven of eight passes, Dallas ran a cold-bloodedly efficient nine-minute offensive series. Instead of failing at third-down conversions, which they did four out of six times in the first half, the 'Boys were converting. Aikman completed four passes in this drive alone for first downs, one each to Irvin, tight end Jay Novacek and Smith. The fourth was a backbreaker for San Francisco. Third-

and-six from the sixteen, a short shot again to Smith, who glided in for the score. It was 24-13. 12:24 left for the Cowboys to complete one of the most improbable seasons in NFL history.

Steve Young tried to answer, but linebacker Ken Norton, Jr., the leading tackler on the NFL's best defense, intercepted and returned the ball to the Niners' 44.

A telling moment was in the offing. Emmitt Smith, behind an offensive line clearly beginning to dominate the older, tiring 49ers, ran 28 yards on the first play after Norton's interception. At fourth and one from the seven, Coach Jimmy Johnson made a shocking decision: Go for it. A field goal would have forced the Niners to score two touchdowns to tie. It was the logical, safe call to make. Let them come to us, put the pressure elsewhere.

Johnson said, in effect, the heck with safe, and went for the first down. Smith was stopped for no gain by Mike Walter. A backfire, and a very loud one if the game

turned into a loss. After the game Johnson said, "If we'd lost the game I would have been the goat. Well, I'm no goat."

It was a piece of strategy, a philosophy, that typified Johnson's and his team's approach to the game. Be unafraid, be bold. The opposition understood Johnson's reasoning only too well. "They kept going for the jugular," wide-out John Taylor said. This time it didn't work. That didn't make the philosophy wrong.

But it did make for some nervous moments. Would the 49ers mount yet another storybook finish?

Young threw everything he had into the air. Joe Montana, God-on-the-sidelines, couldn't have done it better. Completing seven of eight, just as his counterpart had done earlier, Young moved 93 yards. The finale was fitting, a pass to the ethereal Jerry Rice. Five yards for the score. 24-20. 4:22 left. It would not have been entirely unreasonable if some were suggesting a goat-horn fitting.

Jugular time had arrived again. Ball on the Cowboy 21-yard line, first and 10. Use the clock, babe, time on our side. Another no-brainer. Johnson and Norv Turner conferred, Jimmy saying, "Do what is necessary."

Turner went for the throat. It would be the play the game. Maybe of the season. A risky slant-in pass to Alvin Harper turned into a 70-yard 49er heartbreaker. Seven yards later, the Cowboys were looking at Pasadena. When Aikman threw six yards to quicksilver Kelvin Martin for a touchdown, the looking was over. The blocked extra point didn't even matter. The Dallas Cowboys were heading toward the Rose Bowl. The final was 30-20. Young Ken Norton said, "It's almost hard to believe."

It had taken 13 years. "I knew it was going to happen," said 10-year veteran Jim Jeffcoat between smiles. "I knew it was going to happen. I just didn't know when." Somebody else thought they knew how, or at least how much. Before the game, Dave Wannstedt sidled over to Troy Aikman and said, "Get

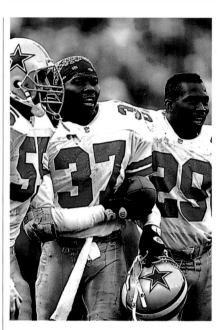

us 21 points. We're not giving up more than 20."

In the dead, eerie silence of the 49er locker room, tackle Harris Barton tried and failed to hide the pain. "It's a brutal deal," the big lineman said softly, "brutal."

The scene in the Cowboy locker room was nearly as classic as the game. The enthusiasm was collegiate...or maybe Pop Warner. Professional athletes, cool and controlled? Forgeddaboutit. It was raucous and loud and gleeful.

Coach Johnson—his face providing the definition of the word "beaming"—climbed onto a chair. "I don't mean to put a damper on anything," he began, causing his team to break into peals of laughter, "but we do have...one...more...game...to play." The room burst into roars. Johnson beamed wider and continued: "Fantastic, fantastic, fantastic." He bubbled on about hard work, training camp in Austin and finished up with a line that has become the team rallying cry: "How 'bout them Cowboys!"

Keys to the game? Troy Aikman, brilliantly coming of age in his fourth season, had put together a nearly perfect game of football. His statistics were as sweet as his touch: 24 for 34, 322 yards, 2 touchdowns, no interceptions. Emmitt Smith, the best back in the game, had behaved similarly: 24 carries, 114 rushing yards and a touchdown—and for

"We do have one more game to play."
–Jimmy Johnson

good measure 7 catches for 59 yards and another TD.

When the battle ended, turnovers would reflect the reality on the field. Four turnovers for the Niners, none for the 'Boys. The Cowboys had pushed the Niners into self-destruction.

With a bold, aggressive, gambling style, Jimmy Johnson had taken his young Cowboys to the mountaintop.

THE GLORY
AND
THE DREAM:

SUPER BOWL CHAMPIONS

The sideline party started earlier than anybody might've imagined, and it didn't want to quit. Everywhere you looked were the sights and sounds of jubilation. Players were hugging. They were laughing. Here was Troy Aikman, smiling a contented smile. There was Emmitt Smith, carrying on with some of his offensive linemen, and not far away, Michael Irvin and Alvin Harper, pass-catching heroes, reveling in their trips to the end zone. Jerry Jones, the owner, seemed to have glee pouring out of every thread of his suit. He did his share of hugging, too.

"THE GREATEST FEELING IN THE WORLD."
–JIMMY JOHNSON

The Rose Bowl clock said that there were still more than 10 minutes to play in Super Bowl XXVII. The sun was just now dipping below the San Gabriel mountains. There was no longer any use in pretending. Cowboys kept turning up in the end zone. The officials were hoisting their arms overhead so often the wonder was they didn't do shoulder damage. Finally even Jimmy Johnson, the architect of the greatest football turnabout in history, couldn't deny it, either. Johnson is a driven man, even by the workaholic standards of the NFL coaching fraternity. Lightening up is not something that comes easily to him — surely not when a Super Bowl game is ongoing. But gradually the steely game-day visage began to soften. It was okay to get a head start on the basking. A couple of players helped him along, sneaking up on Johnson and rubbing their hands all over his head, messing up what has become the most famous hair in sports.

"We said all year that our best game was going to be the last game of the year," Jimmy Johnson said a little while later, hair back in place. Not a dissenting voice was heard.

"I can't sit here and put it in words how I feel," Michael Irvin said. "You dream about the moment. You dream about what it

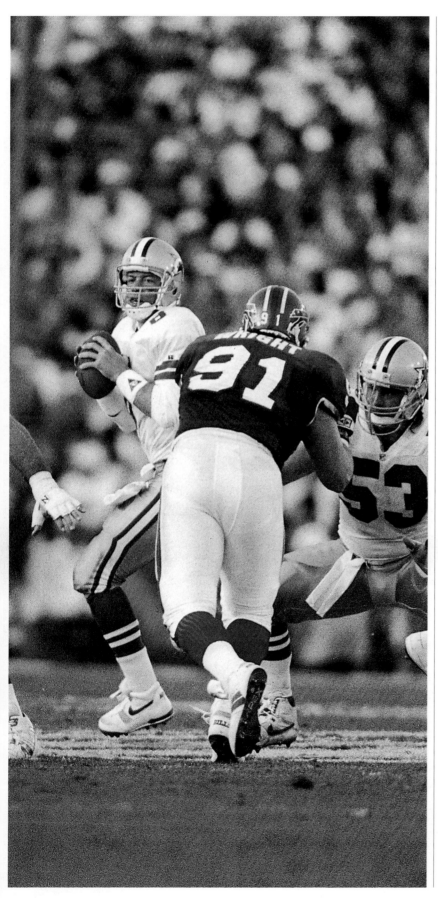

would be like. It's a fantasy. You go through the regular season, the playoffs, and then the game, and it's a dream. Then you win it and it becomes reality. It's something you can't put into words. "It's just great," Irvin said.

Three years removed from the ignominy of 1-15, their worst record ever, the Dallas Cowboys capped an astonishing climb back to the top of the football mountain with a 52-17 rout of the Buffalo Bills. The date was January 31, 1993, and though this storied franchise has been to six Super Bowls now, and had won two previously, it may go down as the most remarkable occasion in the club's 32-year history.

This, after all, was the youngest team in the NFL, one that was up against a Bills team that was making an unprecedented third straight Super Bowl appearance. Never mind that the Bills had dropped the first two. Experience in the ultimate pressure-cooker had to count for something. Didn't it?

"All week long we heard about the experience factor," Harper said. "Well, experience don't matter when you've got football players like the Dallas Cowboys got."

He has a point. The Cowboy heroes truly were too many to name. Emmitt Smith, the league's leading rusher two years running, carved up Buffalo for 108 yards on 22 carries. Irvin had six catches for 114 yards and a pair of touchdowns, and tight end Jay Novacek had seven for 72, including the Cowboys' first score, a 23-yard over-the-middle strike from Aikman. There also was the swarming toughness of the league's No. 1 rated defense, which had much to do with nine Buffalo turnovers, a Super Bowl record. The defense bent some, to be sure. But when did it ever break?

Still, the brightest Dallas star was Aikman, the 26-year-old Oklahoman with the rocket arm and aw-shucks manner. The week before the game, Aikman turned down an invitation from Jay Leno so he could be sure to get a nap in. There was nothing low-key about his numbers in The Game: 22-for-

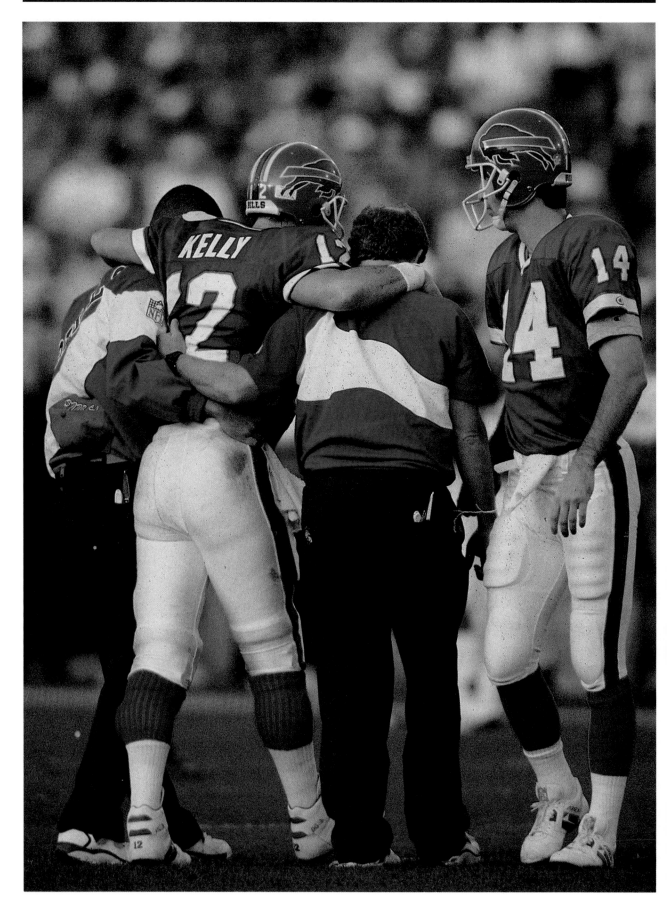

30, 273 yards, four touchdowns. He completed his postseason without throwing an interception in 89 attempts. Aikman's poise and accuracy made his effort worthy of comparison to even the best days of Roger Staubach. He had to deal with the MVP Trophy and 1993 Buick Park Avenue Ultra, even if it made him squirm a bit.

"I'm a little bashful receiving it because we have so many great players," Aikman said. "It really is a shame they have to pick one guy."

"He was smooth. Smooth operator. The best," said Nate Newton, Aikman's 330-pound protector.

With the way things ended, it was easy to forget that neither Aikman nor the Cowboys got off to a particularly auspicious start. A blocked Mike Saxon punt gave Buffalo an early 7-0 lead. The Cowboys went nowhere with their first two drives. Aikman looked shaky. "I think we got caught up in the moment a little bit," Aikman said.

Buffalo was marching again before defensive back James Washington picked off a Kelly pass at the Bills' 48. Smith was pinned for a yard loss, then lost five more on a swing pass. It was third-and-16. Irvin ran a square-in. Aikman, getting time, drilled it perfectly for a 20-yard gain. You could almost feel the play jolt the Cowboys to life. When Aikman found Novacek on the 23-yarder, the score was knotted at seven.

The Cowboy juggernaut was just getting cranked up. By halftime their lead was 28-10. Twice they staggered the Bills with combinations: two TDs within a Super-Bowl-record 15 seconds, then two more within 18 seconds, later in the second quarter. By the time Michael Jackson began his halftime moonwalking, and all that other shenanigans he does, the Bills had the aura of a dazed prizefighter. And why not? You'd be reeling, too.

Moments after Novacek got the Cowboys on the board, the first

Cowboy combination ended with Charles Haley crunching Kelly from the blind side. The ball popped in the air, into the arms of Jimmie Jones, who was in the end zone two yards later. "The ball looked real small coming to me," Jones said. "But it was an easy catch."

The second one-two got started with a 72-yard, five-play march, as methodical as it was rapid. Novacek caught a big pass for nine yards. Smith broke free for 38 yards on a draw play. Irvin spun Bills defensive back Nate Odomes around like a top and caught a 19-yard slant for the TD. The Bills barely had the time to bemoan that before more misfortune hit: Thurman Thomas got stripped by Leon Lett after catching a screen pass. Jimmie Jones pounced on it. Aikman pounced, too, with another strike to Irvin. Rarely has a one-play, 18-yard drive so devastated a team's psyche.

In truth, the Buffalo psyche had already been deeply bruised — by

Back-to-Back Touchdowns

by "The Playmaker"

the Cowboys' aggressive seventeen-man defense. It was the top-ranked unit in the NFL. Who cared if there wasn't a Pro Bowler among them? Early in the second quarter, Kelly had found receiver Andre Reed for a 40-yard gain to the Cowboy four. The Bills were down only 14-7 at the time. Fourteen-all seemed almost a certainty. Fullback Carwell Gardner bulled to the one on first down. On second, Thomas was stuffed by linebacker Vinson Smith. Now it was third-and-goal. Kenneth Davis found a gap over left guard and barreled toward the end zone. Even Kelly started to go up with his arms. And then Ken Norton, Jr. plugged the gap and slammed Davis head on, wrapping him up, throwing him down.

Fourth down. Bills coach Marv Levy decided to go for it. Defensive coordinator Dave Wannstedt, coaching his last game for Jimmy Johnson before taking over his own team in Chicago, called for zone pass coverage. Sure enough, Kelly rolled right, looking to throw. There wasn't much there. He fired to Pete Metzelaars, the tight end. Thomas Everett made a leaping interception. The Bills trudged off with nothing.

The gritty goal-line stand was arguably the game's decisive sequence. Things went from bad to worse for Bills. Norton's clean but wicked hit on Kelly's bad knee ended the quarterback's game midway through the second quarter. The second half provided only more of same: Cowboys churning yards out almost at will, Bills playing a sorry game of butterfingers.

Actually, when Frank Reich, in for Kelly, hooked up with Don Beebe on a 40-yard scoring play to close the third quarter, it made the score 31-17, and gave Buffalo momentary life. Images of the Bills' historic comeback from the 35-3 deficit against the Oilers in the AFC wild card game danced uneasily in Dallas minds. But the Cowboys are not the Oilers. That was clear enough. And if the Bills had had a flask of magic potion with them this day, they probably would've dropped it.

When Alvin Harper corraled a

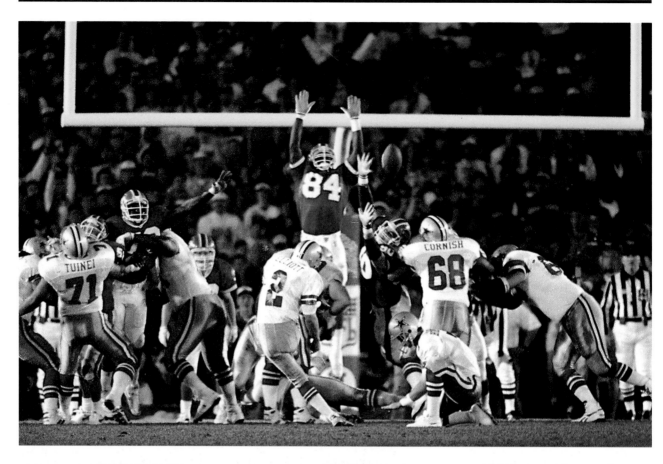

45-yard scoring pass from Aikman to make it 38-17 with just over 10 minutes to play, the outcome was decided. Harper dunked the ball over the goalpost. Everett's second interception set up a Smith eight-yard score, and then Norton scooped up a fumble and ran it in from the nine. By now you were almost hoping the referees could stop it, so embarrassing was this to the Bills.

The only thing that went right at the end for Buffalo came after Leon Lett grabbed a fumble — turnover No. 9 if you're still keeping track — and was a yard away from a 64-yard touchdown when he slowed to a trot, held the ball out — and got caught from behind by the Bills' Beebe. Showing admirable hustle, Beebe punched the ball away, out of the side of the end zone. The touchback prevented the Cowboys from breaking the 49ers' record of 55 Super Bowl points.

That was only the cherry, though. The rest of this Super Bowl sundae, a mountainous treat, was already being savored. Now the sideline party, first for the Cowboys in 15 years, was in full swing. Jimmy Johnson's hair got messed up a few more times, once by the traditional ice bath. "I've always known his hair would move," Jerry Jones said. The dancing and cavorting and merriment just went on and on. Once this franchise was led by names like Lilly and Hill, Staubach and Howley, Dorsett and Pearson and so many others. Now the names are Aikman and Smith, Irvin and Norton, Harper and Novacek — and for sure, so many others. The clock finally wound its way down. The hurt and humiliation of 1-15 were dissolving with the Pasadena daylight.

This unimaginably fast trip to glory was complete, and all over the country, millions of fans of the Dallas Cowboys were joining the celebration in their own right, in living rooms and bar rooms, in the streets, and in other places, too — such as Cliff Temple Baptist Church in the Oak Cliff section of Dallas. Cliff Temple has a weekly

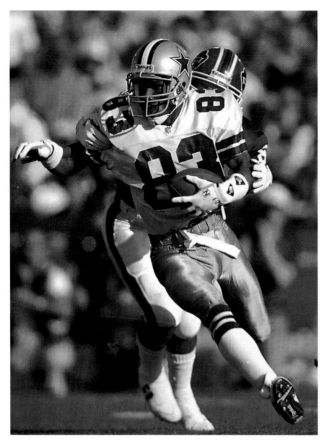

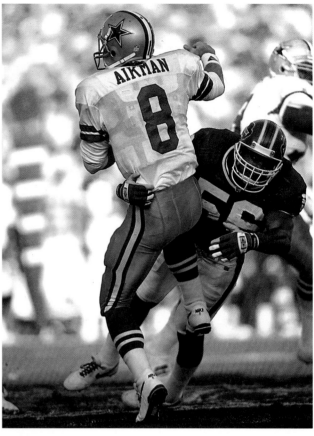

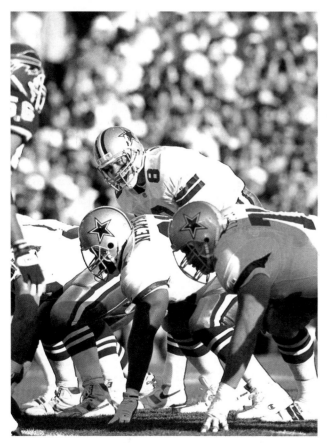

service at 6 p.m. on Sunday night. On Sunday, January 31, 1993, they opted to have a Super Bowl party instead. According to *The Dallas Morning News*, about 100 Cliff Temple churchgoers donned Cowboy sweatshirts. A 9-foot-by-12-foot screen was set up. The experience turned out to be almost divine in its own right. "We just wanted to have a good time with it. That's spiritual enough," pastor Dean Dickens said. To which the Dallas Cowboys might have said: Amen.

A COWBOY CHRONOLOGY

Jan. 28, 1960:   The Dallas Cowboys franchise is awarded to Clint Murchison, Jr. and Bedford Wynne.

Aug. 6, 1960:   The Cowboys lose to San Francisco in their first preseason game.

Aug. 27, 1960:   Frank Clarke catches two long touchdown passes to lead the Cowboys to their first win against the New York Giants, 14-3.

Sept. 17, 1961:   Dallas clinches a victory from Pittsburgh at the Cotton Bowl with a 27-yard field goal. It's the Cowboys' first NFL regular-season victory.

Oct. 14, 1962:   Amos Marsh returns a kickoff 101 yards, and fellow Cowboy Mike Gaechter returns an interception 100 yards for fourth-quarter touchdowns. It is the first time in NFL history two 100-yard plays are made in the same game. The host Cowboys defeat Philadelphia, 41-19.

July 12, 1963:   The Lutheran College training camp in Thousand Oaks, California, is opened.

Feb. 5, 1964:   Coach Tom Landry signs a 10-year contract extension.

Dec. 18, 1966:   The Cowboys defeat the New York Giants 17-7 to earn their first Eastern Conference title. The Cowboys finish the season 10-3-1.

Jan. 1, 1967:   The Cowboys are defeated 34-27 by Green Bay in their first NFL Championship Game.

Dec. 23, 1967:   Owner Clint Murchison announces he plans to build Texas Stadium outside of Irving.

Dec. 31, 1967:   The sub-zero NFL Championship Game known as the "Ice Bowl." Green Bay defeats the Cowboys, 21-17.

Jan. 5, 1969:   On the heels of defeat in the Eastern Championship game against Cleveland, the Cowboys beat Minnesota 17-3 to win the Playoff Bowl.

Jan. 25, 1969:   Groundbreaking for Texas Stadium.

July 25, 1969:   Don Meredith, the team's quarterback and the last member of the original Cowboys, announces his retirement.

July 18, 1969:   Don Perkins, the team's all-time rushing leader, retires.

Jan. 17, 1971:   Dallas' first Super Bowl. A field goal by Jim O'Brien ekes out a 16-13 victory for Baltimore.

Oct. 24, 1971:   The Cowboys "break in" Texas Stadium with a 44-21 victory over New England.

Jan. 16, 1972:   Super Bowl VI. Roger Staubach quarterbacks the team past Miami, 24-3, with two touchdown passes.

Dec. 29, 1972:   Calvin Hill rushes for 111 yards to become the first Cowboy running back to gain 1,000 yards in a season. Hill finishes the season with 1,036 yards.

Dec. 31, 1972:   Washington defeats Dallas in the NFC title game, 26-3, after the Cowboys reach the playoffs for a record seventh consecutive season.

Sept. 24, 1973:   Coach Landry and the 'Boys defeat New Orleans with a 40-3 victory, the team's 100th victory.

Nov. 23, 1975:   Bob Lilly, former defensive tackle, is the first inductee into the Cowboys' Ring of Honor.

Dec. 28, 1975:   The Cowboys clinch a 17-14 first-round playoff-game victory against Minnesota with Roger Staubach's 50-yard "Hail Mary" touchdown pass to Drew Pearson.

Jan. 18, 1976:	The Cowboys are defeated by Pittsburgh, 21-17, in Super Bowl X.
Nov. 7, 1976:	Don Meredith and Don Perkins are inducted into the Ring of Honor.
Oct. 30, 1977:	Chuck Howley is inducted into the Ring of Honor.
Jan. 1, 1978:	The Cowboys take home their fourth NFC Championship with a 23-6 victory over Minnesota.
Jan. 15, 1978:	Super Bowl XII. The Cowboys beat, Denver 27-10.
Jan. 7, 1979:	The Cowboys ride into their record fifth Super Bowl with a 28-0 playoff victory against Los Angeles. It is their 13th consecutive winning season.
Jan. 21, 1979:	Super Bowl XIII. Terry Bradshaw leads Pittsburgh to a 35-31 victory against Dallas.
Dec. 30, 1979:	In their 20th NFL season, Dallas makes the playoffs for the 13th time in 14 years. The season ends with a 21-19 loss to Los Angeles.
Mar. 30, 1980:	After 11 years with the Cowboys, quarterback Roger Staubach retires.
Aug. 2, 1980:	Bob Lilly is inducted into the Pro Football Hall of Fame.
Dec 21, 1980:	Dallas wraps up its 15th consecutive winning season with a 35-27 victory over Philadelphia to get into the playoffs.
Dec. 28, 1980:	A 34-13 playoff victory over Los Angeles earns Tom Landry his 200th victory as coach. Curly Lambeau, George Halas and Landry are the only NFL coaches with 200 victories.
Jan. 11, 1981:	Dallas is defeated 20-7 by Philadelphia in the NFC title game.
Oct. 25, 1981:	Mel Renfro is inducted into the Ring of Honor.
Jan. 10, 1982:	The Catch. With 51 seconds left, Dwight Clark snares 6-yard touchdown pass from Joe Montana to help San Francisco eke out a 28-27 victory over Dallas in the NFC Championship Game.
Dec. 13, 1982:	Dallas takes home its 17th consecutive winning season with a 37-7 win over Houston.
Oct. 9, 1983:	Roger Staubach is inducted into the Ring Of Honor.
Nov. 6, 1983:	An 18th consecutive winning season is insured with a 27-20 victory over Philadelphia.
Nov. 29, 1983:	Ground is broken for Valley Ranch, the Cowboys' new training facility in Irving.
Mar. 19, 1984:	Sale of the Dallas Cowboys to a limited partnership headed by H.R. "Bum" Bright is okayed by NFL owners.
May 18, 1984:	Bright's purchase of the Cowboys is completed. The cost? $60 million for the Cowboys, plus a 65-year lease on Texas Stadium for $20 million.
Dec. 2, 1984:	Dallas wraps up its 19th consecutive winning season with a 26-10 win against Philadelphia.
Aug. 3, 1985:	Roger Staubach is inducted into the Pro Football Hall Of Fame.
Oct. 13, 1985:	Tony Dorsett becomes the sixth player in NFL history to rush for 10,000 yards in a career with a 19-yard run against Pittsburgh.
Nov. 24, 1985:	A win against Philadelphia clinches a 20th consecutive winning season, an NFL record.

March 30, 1987:	Clint Murchison, Jr., the founder of the Dallas Cowboys, dies.
Dec. 20, 1987:	Tony Dorsett rushes past the 12,000-yard mark for career rushing with a 52-yard run against Los Angeles.
Sept. 12, 1988:	Tom Landry's 29th consecutive season with Dallas. Only Green Bay's Curly Lambeau has coached an NFL team as long as Landry.
Feb. 25, 1989:	Arkansas oilman Jerry Jones buys the Dallas Cowboys from H.R. Bright. Jones announces that Tom Landry will be replaced by University of Miami coach Jimmy Johnson.
April 18, 1989:	Tex Schramm, Cowboys president and general manager, announces his resignation.
July 18, 1990:	Dallas opens its St. Edward's University training camp in Austin.
Aug. 4, 1990:	Tom Landry is inducted into the Pro Football Hall of Fame.
Sept. 9, 1991:	Dallas is defeated by Washington in their first "Monday Night Football" appearance since November 1987. The game draws one the largest televison audiences of the year.
Sept. 29, 1991:	The Cowboys defeat the Super Bowl Champion New York Giants 21-16 at Texas Stadium.
Nov. 24, 1991:	Dallas cuts short an 11-game Washington winning streak with a 24-21 victory.
Dec. 15, 1991:	Dallas makes it to the playoffs for the first time since 1985 with a 25-13 victory over Philadelphia.
Dec. 21, 1991:	Dallas finishes the 1991 season with its best record in eight years, an 11-5 record. It is the 11th time in Cowboy history that the team has won 11 games or more.
Dec. 29, 1992:	Dallas has its first playoff win since 1982 with a 17-13 victory against Chicago.
Jan. 5, 1992:	Dallas loses to Detroit in the Divisonal Playoffs, 38-6.
Dec. 21, 1992:	Dallas clinches first NFC East title since 1985 with a 41-17 Monday Night rout of Atlanta.
Jan. 10, 1993:	The Cowboys ride past Philadelphia in the NFC Divisional playoffs with a 34-10 victory.
Jan. 17, 1993:	Dallas Cowboys beat San Francisco, 30-20, in the NFC Championship Game.
Jan. 31, 1993:	Super Bowl XXVII. The Dallas Cowboys defeat the Buffalo Bills 52-17 in a record-breaking sixth Super Bowl appearance.

A LOOK BACK AT PREVIOUS COWBOY SUPER BOWL GAMES

SUPER BOWL V
Baltimore 16
Dallas 13

The first Super Bowl under the new merger of the NFL and the AFL ended in high drama, but only after both teams suffered through 60 minutes of turnovers. The Baltimore Colts fumbled five times (losing three) and suffered three interceptions. The Cowboys lost one fumble and threw three interceptions.

With Dallas leading 6-0 in the second quarter, Johnny Unitas threw a pass off the fingertips of both receiver Eddie Hinton and defensive back Mel Renfro... into the waiting arms of tight end John Mackey, who sped all the way for a 75-yard score.

Dallas regained the lead before the half on a seven-yard pass from Craig Morton to Duane Thomas. The lead stood until the fourth quarter when Rich Volk picked off a Morton pass, setting up the tying touchdown scored by Tom Nowatzke.

Then, with 1:09 to play, linebacker Mike Curtis picked off another Morton pass on the Cowboys' 28. Three plays later rookie kicker Jim O'Brien, who had an extra point blocked earlier, booted a 32-yard field goal to give the Colts a 16-13 win. Dallas Chuck Howley, who picked off two passes, became the first defensive player and the first player from a losing team to be named Most Valuable Player.

SUPER BOWL VI
Dallas 24
Miami 3

After a near-miss in Super Bowl V, the Cowboys thoroughly dominated the Miami Dolphins. Led by Duane Thomas, the Cowboys used a punishing ground attack in setting a Super Bowl record of 252 yards rushing.

Leading only 10-3 at the half, the Cowboys marched 71 yards to start the third quarter and scored on a three-yard run by Thomas, who finished the game with 95 yards on 19 carries.

Chuck Howley's interception of a Bob Griese pass set up Dallas' final score—a pass from from Staubach to Ditka. Dallas controlled the ball most of the game, running 69 offensive plays to Miami's 44 plays.

Miami became the first team not to score a touchdown in a Super Bowl. Staubach was voted the team's Most Valuable Player. He completed 12 of 19 passes for 119 yards and two scores.

SUPER BOWL X
Pittsburgh 21
Dallas 17

Super Bowl X will be forever known as Swann's Song. Favorite Pittsburgh was present for the second consecutive year. Dallas was the first wildcard team to ever reach the NFL final game.

But, unexpectedly, Dallas held a 10-7 lead. Then late in the game reserve Steeler running back made a huge play, blocking Mitch Hoope's punt at the Dallas nine. The ball bounded in the end zone. Safety, score 10-9. It seemed the turning point.

Roy Gerela kicked two field goals, then with the score 15-10, Lynn Swnn took a 59-yard pass from Terry Bradshaw and ran five more yards into the end zone.

The stage was set for a thrilling finale. With less than two minutes to go, the Cowboys marched 80 yards in just five plays to draw close at 21-17. During the drive quarterback Roger Staubach made two crucial throws, and Drew Pearson made two crucial catches.

On Pittsburgh last series, with Terry Hanratty in for the injured Bradshw, the Cowboys stopped the Steelers with less than a minute and half left. First and 10, Dallas on their own 43.

But Staubach and company couldn't mount a game-saving drive. Five plays later Pittsburgh had won Super Bowl X.

SUPER BOWL XII
Dallas 27
Denver 10

The Cowboys evened their Super Bowl record 2-2 by taking advantage of eight Bronco turnovers. Dallas converted two interceptions into 10 points and Efren Herera's 35-yard field goal made it a 13-0 halftime advantage.

Denver's Jim Turner then kicked a 47-yard field goal. But later in the third quarter, Dallas wide receiver Butch Johnson made a diving catch in the end-zone to complete a 45-yard touchdown pass from Roger Staubach and put the Cowboys ahead 20-3.

Denver again cut the lead, 20-10, this time on a one-yard run by Rob Lytle. But with 7:04 to play fullback Robert Newhouse tossed a 29-yard option pass to Golden Richards for the final score of the game.

Staubach completed 17 of 25 passes for 183 yards with no interceptions and Tony Dorsett gained 66 yards on 15 carries.

For the first time there were co-MVPs of the Super Bowl. The award was shared by defensive linemen Randy White and Harvey Martin of Dallas.

SUPER BOWL XIII
Pittsburgh 35
Dallas 31

Terry Bradshaw threw four touchdown passes to lead the Steelers to their third Super Bowl win in as many tries. Bradshaw, voted the game's MVP, completed 17 of 30 passes for 318 yards breaking Bart Starr's record of 250 yards' passing by halftime.

Two Bradshaw-to-John Stallworth and one Bradshaw-to-Rocky Bleier scored in the first half to give Pittsburgh a 21-14 lead at halftime.

Franco Harris rambled 22 yards for a score after Rafeal Septein had cut Pittsburgh's lead to 21-17 with a three-pointer. Pittsburgh then seemingly put the game out of reach with less than seven minutes to play when Bradshaw hit Lynn Swann for an 18-yard strike to make the score 35-17.

Roger Staubach threw his second scoring pass of the game with 2:23 left, a seven yarder to Billy Joe Dupree. The Cowboys then recovered an onside kick and scored again on Staubach's third touchdown pass with 22 seconds remaining.

Dallas' bid for another onside kick recovery failed as Bleier fell on the ball with 17 seconds left.

THE RING OF HONOR: A COWBOY TRADITION OF GREATNESS

The Dallas Cowboys remember players who contributed to the team's greatness with extraordinary feats on the gridiron. Their names can be seen in silver on the wall below the Texas Stadium press box. The Ring Of Honor includes:

BOB LILLY

Texas E. Schramm, Dallas' first general manager, had Gil Brandt scout for the Cowboys where they were still a young club in the NFL. Brandt looked for talent among college seniors and he found it in 1961. The talent was 6 feet four inches and weighed in at 251 pounds. Who was this bright young performer? Bob Lilly—an end for Texas Christian, where he was two-time All SWC pick and All-America. Lilly was the Cowboys' first draft choice and became a defensive tackle. He was the club's first inductee to the Ring Of Honor in 1975. Later, in 1980, he was Dallas' first inductee into the Pro Football Hall Of Fame. Lilly was a seven-time All-Pro and played in a record 11 Pro Bowls.

DON MEREDITH

"Dandy" Don Meredith, out of Southern Methodist quarterbacked the Cowboys from 1960 to 1968. He led the team to their first winning season. At SMU, Meredith was a two-time All-American. In 1966, he was named NFL Player of the Year, and he was inducted into the Ring Of Honor in 1976.

DON PERKINS

From 1961 to 1968, Don Perkins served as the Cowboys' running back. He was the first Cowboy to surpass the 6,000-yard mark for rushing. Like Meredith, Perkins was signed before Dallas was given its NFL franchise. In each of his eight seasons, Perkins was listed among the NFL's leading ten rushers. He was a six-time Pro Bowl selection and was named NFL Rookie of the Year in 1961 and All-Pro in 1962. Perkins was brought into the Ring Of Honor in 1976.

CHUCK HOWLEY

"I don't know that I've seen anybody better at linebacker than Howley," Tom Landry said upon Howley's retirement. Howley played with the Cowboys from 1961 to 1972. He was a six-time All-Pro and the MVP in Super Bowl V. Howley was an All-America center at West Virginia; he was snapped up by Chicago who traded him to Dallas. Dallas brought Howley, a six-time Pro Bowl selection, into the Ring Of Honor in 1977.

MEL RENFRO

Mel Renfro started out as a world-class sprinter and All-American halfback at Oregon. With the Cowboys, Renfro had a 26.4-yard career average as a kickoff returner and was the team's all-time interceptor. Renfro was named to the Pro Bowl in his first 10 NFL seasons and was a five-time All Pro. He was inducted into the Ring Of Honor in 1981.

ROGER STAUBACH

Roger Staubach was well on his way to greatness as quarterback at the Naval Academy, where he won the Heisman Trophy and the Maxwell Award. Drafted in 1964, Staubach was the team's quarterback from 1969 to 1979. Staubach led the Cowboys to two Super Bowl titles, four Super Bowls and six NFC Championship Games. In 1983, Staubach was inducted into the Ring Of Honor and later, in 1985, he was elected into the Pro Football Hall Of Fame.

LEE ROY JORDAN

Lee Roy Jordan played linebacker for the Dallas Cowboys from 1963 to 1976. He was a first-round draft choice from Alabama, where he was an All-American linebacker. Jordan was named to the Pro Bowl five times and All-Pro twice. Dallas inducted Jordan into the Ring Of Honor in 1989.

The Jones/Johnson Era: Wins and Losses

1989 (1-15)

Sept.	09	L	0	New Orleans	28
Sept.	17	L	21	Atlanta	27
Sept.	24	L	7	Washington	30
Oct.	01	L	13	N.Y. Giants	30
Oct.	08	L	13	Green Bay	31
Oct.	15	L	14	San Francisco	31
Oct.	22	L	28	Kansas City	36
Oct.	29	L	10	Phoenix	19
Nov.	05	W	13	Washington	3
Nov.	12	L	20	Phoenix	24
Nov.	19	L	14	Miami	17
Nov.	23	L	0	Philadelphia	27
Dec.	03	L	31	L.A. Rams	35
Dec.	10	L	10	Philadelphia	20
Dec.	16	L	0	N.Y. Giants	15
Dec.	24	L	10	Green Bay	20

1990 (7-9)

Sept.	09	W	17	San Diego	14
Sept.	16	L	7	N.Y. Giants	28
Sept.	23	L	15	Washington	19
Sept.	30	L	17	N.Y. Giants	31
Oct.	07	W	14	Tampa Bay	10
Oct.	14	L	3	Phoenix	20
Oct.	21	W	17	Tampa Bay	13
Oct.	28	L	20	Philadelphia	21
Nov.	04	L	9	N.Y. Jets	24
Nov.	11	L	6	San Francisco	24
Nov.	18	W	24	L.A. Rams	21
Nov.	22	W	27	Washington	17
Dec.	02	W	17	New Orleans	13
Dec.	16	W	41	Phoenix	10
Dec.	23	L	3	Philadelphia	17
Dec.	30	L	7	Atlanta	26

1991 (11-5)

Sept.	01	W	26	Cleveland	14
Sept.	09	L	31	Washington	33
Sept.	15	L	0	Philadelphia	24
Sept.	22	W	17	Phoenix	9
Sept.	29	W	21	N.Y. Giants	16
Oct.	06	W	20	Green Bay	17
Oct.	13	W	35	Cincinnati	23
Oct.	27	L	10	Detroit	34
Nov.	03	W	27	Phoenix	7
Nov.	10	L	23	Houston	26
Nov.	17	L	9	N.Y. Giants	22
Nov.	24	W	24	Washington	21
Nov.	28	W	20	Pittsburgh	10
Dec.	08	W	23	New Orleans	14
Dec.	15	W	25	Philadelphia	13
Dec.	22	W	31	Atlanta	27

1991 First Round Playoffs
(Chicago)

Dec.	29	W	17	Chicago	13

1991 Divisional Playoffs
(Detroit)

Jan.	05	L	6	Detroit	38

1992 (15-3)

Sept.	07	W	23	Washington	10
Sept.	13	W	34	N.Y. Giants	28
Sept.	20	W	31	Phoenix	20
Oct.	05	L	7	Philadelphia	31
Oct.	11	W	27	Seattle	0
Oct.	18	W	17	Kansas City	10
Oct.	25	W	28	L.A. Raiders	13
Nov.	01	W	20	Philadelphia	10
Nov.	08	W	37	Detroit	3
Nov.	15	L	23	L.A. Rams	27
Nov.	22	W	16	Phoenix	10
Nov.	26	W	30	N.Y. Giants	3
Dec.	06	W	31	Denver	27
Dec.	13	L	17	Washington	20
Dec.	21	W	41	Atlanta	17
Dec.	27	W	27	Chicago	14

1992 First Round Playoffs
(Dallas)

Jan.	10	W	34	Philadelphia	10

1992 Divisional Playoffs
(San Francisco)

Jan.	17	W	30	San Francisco	20

1992 Super Bowl
(Pasadena)

Jan.	31	W	52	Buffalo	17

THE 1992-93 SEASON: PRE-SUPER BOWL STATISTICS

SCORING

Player	TD Run	TD Rec	TD Ret	EP M-A	FG M-A	Pts Pts
Elliot	0	0	0	47-48	24-35	119
Playoffs	0	0	0	7-8	3-4	16
E. Smith	18	1	0	0-0	0-0	114
Playoffs	2	1	0	0-0	0-0	18
Irvin	0	7	0	0-0	0-0	42
Novacek	0	6	0	0-0	0-0	36
Playoffs	0	1	0	0-0	0-0	6
Martin	0	3	2	0-0	0-0	30
Playoffs	0	1	0	0-0	0-0	6
Harper	0	4	0	0-0	0-0	24
Johnston	0	2	0	0-0	0-0	12
Playoffs	1	0	0	0-0	0-0	6
Aikman	1	0	0	0-0	0-0	6
Horton	0	0	0	0-0	0-0	6
Maryland	0	0	0	0-0	0-0	6
Williams	0	0	0	0-0	0-0	6
Holt	0	0	0	0-0	0-0	2
Gainer	0	0	0	0-0	0-0	0
Playoffs	1	0	0	0-0	0-0	6
Tennell	0	0	0	0-0	0-0	0
Playoffs	0	1	0	0-0	0-0	6
Other	1	0	0	0-0	0-0	6
Totals	20	23	5	47-48	24-35	409
Playoffs	4	4	0	7-3	3-4	64
Opponents	11	16	2	27-29	14-17	243
Playoffs	1	2	0	3-3	3-4	30

PASSING

Player	Att	Cm	Yds	TD	Int	Lng
Aikman	473	302	3445	23	14	87
Playoffs	59	39	522	4	0	70
Beuerlein	18	12	152	0	1	27
Totals	491	314	3597	23	15	87
Playoffs	59	39	522	4	0	70
Opponents	484	283	3036	16	17	81
Playoffs	85	42	473	2	2	36

RUSHING

Player	No	Yds	Avg	Lng	TD
E. Smith	373	1713	4.6	68	18
Playoffs	49	228	4.7	28	2
Aikman	37	105	2.8	19	1
Playoffs	6	10	1.7	8	0
D. Johnston	17	61	3.6	14	0
Playoffs	3	11	3.7	4	1

Player	No	Yds	Avg	Lng	TD
Agee	16	54	3.4	10	1
Harper	1	15	15.0	15	0
Playoffs	1	3	3.0	3	0
Martin	2	13	6.5	8	0
Beuerlein	4	-7	-1.7	-1	0
Irvin	1	-9	-9.0	-9	0
Gainer	0	0	0.0	0	0
Playoffs	9	29	3.2	0	1
Other	49	176	3.6	15	1.0
Totals	500	2121	4.2	681	20
Playoffs	88	281	4.1	28	4
Opponents	345	1244	3.6	29	11
Playoffs	38	177	4.7	16	1

RECEIVING

Player	No	Yds	Avg	Lng	TD
Irvin	78	1396	17.9	87	7
Playoffs	12	174	14.5	33	0
Novacek	68	630	9.3	34	6
Playoffs	6	64	10.7	20	1
E. Smith	59	335	5.7	26	1
Playoffs	7	59	8.4	16	1
Harper	35	562	16.1	52	4
Playoffs	4	158	39.5	70	0
Martin	32	359	11.2	27	3
Playoffs	4	33	8.3	12	1
Johnston	32	249	7.8	18	2
Playoffs	5	33	6.6	10	0
Roberts	3	36	12.0	18	0
Agee	3	18	6.0	8	0
Gesek	1	4	4.0	4	0
Tennell	0	0	0.0	0	0
Playoffs	1	1	1.0	1	1
Other	3	8	2.7	6	0
Totals	314	3597	11.5	87	23
Playoffs	39	522	13.4	70	4
Opponents	263	3036	11.5	81	18
Playoffs	42	473	11.3	36	2

INTERCEPTIONS

Player	No	Yds	Avg	Lng	TD
J. Washington	3	31	10.3	16	0
Playoffs	1	21	21.0	21	0
Gant	3	19	6.3	11	0
Everett	2	28	14.0	17	0
Horton	2	15	7.5	15	1
Holt	2	11	5.5	8	0
K. Smith	2	10	5.0	7	0
L. Brown	1	30	30.0	30	0
Myles	1	13	13.0	13	0
Harper	1	1	1.0	1	0
Norton	0	0	0.0	0	0
Playoffs	1	14	14.0	14	0
Totals	17	158	9.3	30	1
Playoffs	2	35	17.5	21	0
Opponents	15	300	20.0	50	0
Playoffs	0	0	0 0	0	0

PUNTING

Player	Gross No	Net Yds	Avg.	Avg.	Lng
Saxon	61	2620	43.0	33.5	58
Playoffs	8	314	39.3	32.5	50
Totals	61	2620	43.0	33.5	
Playoffs	8	314	39.3	32.5	50
Opponents	87	3660	42.1	35.1	73
Playoffs	8	343	42.9	38.8	57

PUNT RETURNS

Player	No	FC	Yds	Avg.	Lng	TD
Martin	42	18	532	12.7	79	2
Playoffs	2	1	13	6.5	8	0
Horton	1	0	1	1.0	1	0
K. Smith	1	0	17	17.0	17	0
J. Washington	0	0	0	0.0	0	0
Playoffs	1	0	0	0.0	0	0
Totals	44	18	550	12.5	79	2
Playoffs	3	1	13	4.3	8	0
Opponents	54	6	397	11.7	65	0
Playoffs	7	1	54	7.7	15	0

KICKOFF RETURNS

Player	No	Yds	Avg	Lng	TD
Martin	24	503	21.0	59	0
Playoffs	5	122	24.4	39	0
Holmes	3	70	23.3	28	0
Edwards	1	0	0.0	0	0
K. Smith	1	9	9.0	9	0
Playoffs	1	11	11.0	11	0
Others	8	117	14.6	21	0
Totals	37	699	18.9	59	0
Playoffs	6	133	22.2	39	0
Opponents	60	1217	20.3	42	0
Playoffs	11	224	20.4	50	0

SCORE BY QUARTERS

	1	2	3	4	OT	Total
Dallas	108	116	134	51	0	409
Playoffs	10	17	17	20	0	64
Opponents	54	53	51	85	0	243
Playoffs	10	3	3	14	0	30

SUPER BOWL
Scoring Summary

Bills	07	03	07	00	—17
Cowboys	14	14	3	21	—52

First Quarter:

Bills—Thomas 2-yard run (Christie kick), 5:00. Drive: 16 yards, 4 plays. Key plays: Tasker block of Saxon's punt, ball out-of-bounds on Cowboys' 16. Tolbert's sack of Kelly on 3rd and 3 nullified by def. holding call, giving Bills first down at Cowboys' 5. Bills 7, Cowboys 0.

Cowboys—Novacek 23-yard pass from Aikman (Elliott kick), 13:24. Drive: 47 yards, 6 plays. Keys: Washington interception of Kelly's pass and 13-yard return to Bills' 47; Aikman 20-yard pass to Irvin. Cowboys 7, Bills 7.

Cowboys—J. Jones 2-yard fumble return (Elliott kick), 13:39. Key plays: Haley 8-yard sack of Kelly forces fumble, recovered by J. Jones. Cowboys 14, Bills 7.

Second Quarter:

Bills—FG Christie 21, 11:36. Drive: 82-yards, 12 plays. Key plays: Reich, on first play after replacing injured Kelly, 7-yard pass to Metzelaars on 3rd and 3; Reich 38-yard pass to Reed.
Cowboys 14, Bills 10.

Cowboys—Irvin 19-yard pass from Aikman (Elliott kick), 13:06. Drive: 72 yards, 5 plays. Keys: Aikman 9-yard pass to Novacek; E. Smith 38-yard run.
Cowboys 21, Bills 10.

Cowboys —Irvin 18-yard pass from Aikman (Elliott kick), 13:24. Drive: 18 yards, 1 play. Keys: Thomas fumble on screen pass forced by Lett and recovered by J. Jones at Bills' 18.
Cowboys 28, Bills 10.

Third Quarter:

Cowboys—FG Elliott 20, 6:39. Drive: 77 yards, 12 plays. Keys: E. Smith 11-yard run; Aikman 25 and 12-yard passes to Irvin.
Cowboys 31, Bills 10.

Bills—Beebe 40-yard pass from Reich (Christie kick), 15:00. Drive 61 yards, 5 plays. Keys: K. Davis 12-yard run; Reich 13-yard pass to Reed.
Cowboys 31, Bills 17.

Fourth Quarter

Cowboys—Harper 45-yard pass from Aikman (Elliott kick), 4:56. Drive: 56 yards, 2 plays. Keys: E. Smith 11-yard run.
Cowboys 38, Bills 17.

Cowboys—E. Smith 10-yard run, (Elliott kick), 6:48. Drive: 8 yards, 3 plays. Keys: Everett 22-yard interception return to Bills' 8.
Cowboys 45, Bills 17.

Cowboys—Norton 9-yard fumble return (Elliott kick), 7:29. Cowboys 52, Bills 17.

Individual Statistics

Rushing

Cowboys	E. Smith	22	108 yds
	Aikman	03	28 yds
	Gainer	02	1 yds
	Johnston	01	1 yds
Bills	K. Davis	15	86 yds
	Thomas	11	19 yds
	Gardner	01	01 yds
	Reich	02	00 yds

Passing

Cowboys	Aikman	22	30	00	273 yds
Bills	Kelly	04	07	02	82 yds
	Reich	18	31	02	194 yds

Receiving

Cowboys	Novacek	07	72 yds
	Irvin	06	114 yds
	E.Smith	06	27 yds
	Johnston	02	15 yds
	Harper	01	45 yds
Bills	Reed	08	152 yds
	Thomas	04	10 yds
	K. Davis	03	16 yds
	Beebe	02	50 yds
	Tasker	02	30 yds
	Metzelaars	02	12 yds

Tackles-Assists-Sacks

Cowboys   Norton 8-1-0,   Haley 5-0-1,   Washington 4-2-0,
           Edwards 4-2-0,   Maryland 4-2-0,   Woodson 4-0-0,
           Lett 3-0-1,   Everett 3-0-1,   Holmes 3-0-0,
           Jeffcoat 2-0-1,   Casillas 2-3-0,   Brown 2-0-0,
           V. Smith 2-0-0,   Jones 2-0-0,   Gant 2-1-0,
           Horton 1-0-0,   K. Smith 1-0-0,   Holt 1-0-0,
           Tolbert 1-0-0   Gainer 1-0-0,   Pruitt 1-0-0.

Bills   Bennett 8-1-0,   Talley 6-0-0,   Patton 6-0-0,
           B. Smith 4-1-1,   Odomes 4-0-0,   Conlan 3-5-0,
           Jones 3-2-0,   Williams 3-2-0,   Darby 3-0-0,
           Wright 3-0-0,   Pike 3-0-0,   Kelso 2-2-0,
           Hanson 2-1-0,   Hale 2-0-0,   Maddox 1-0-0.

Interceptions

Cowboys   Everett 2,   Brown, Washington.

Bills   None.

Team Stats

	Bills	Cowboys
First Downs	22	20
Rushing	7	9
Passing	11	11
Penalty	14	0
Third Down Eff.	5-11	5-11
Fourth Down Eff.	0-2	0-1
Total Net Yds.	362	408
Total Plays	71	60
Avg. Gain	5.1	6.8
Net Yds. Rush.	108	137
Rushes	29	29
Avg. Rush	3.7	4.7
Net Yds. Pass	254	271
Compl-Att	22-38	22-30
Yds p. Pass	6.0	8.7
Sack-yd-lost	4-22	1-2
Had intercept.	4	0
Punts-Avg.	3-45	4-33
Total Ret. Yds	90	149
Punt Ret.	1-0	3-35
Kickoff Ret.	4-90	4-79
Intercept.	0-0	4-35
Penalties-Yds	4-30	8-53
Fumbles-Lost	8-5	4-2
Time of Poss.	28:48	31:12